THE EMERGENCE OF MAN

By the Same Author

THE ASCENT OF HUMANITY

The EMERGENCE of

MAN

GERALD HEARD

Decorated by
WILLIAM KERMODE

London · JONATHAN CAPE · Toronto

FIRST PUBLISHED 1931

JONATHAN CAPE LTD., 30 BEDFORD SQUARE, LONDON
AND 91 WELLINGTON STREET WEST, TORONTO
JONATHAN CAPE & HARRISON SMITH INC.
139 EAST 46th STREET, NEW YORK

PRINTED IN GREAT BRITAIN BY J. AND J. GRAY, EDINBURGH
PAPER MADE BY JOHN DICKINSON AND CO. LTD.
BOUND BY A. W. BAIN AND CO. LTD.

CONTENTS

5

INTRODUCTION

Sixty years ago Winwood Read wrote his *Martyrdom of Man*. It was a strange book for that age. Darwin had made men realise that man had ascended and was not a fallen creature. Instead of the medieval vision of 'even Aristotle but a ruined Adam,' there was built up the picture of man becoming slowly perfected out of the ape. Nor were Aristotle and the ancients to be considered the ultimate achievement of humanity. Bacon had inaugurated the modern age of Science with the slogan: 'I reject the Syllogism.' The experimental method which he advocated so powerfully had in a couple of generations placed the frontiers of science considerably beyond where they had stood when Greek speculation ceased, and thereafter the progress had not slackened, but rather had been progressively accelerated. And the critical methods which had proved so fruitful in the physical sciences were also yielding no less hopeful results when applied to history.. Men discovered that something like a science of history could take the place of the old humiliating myth and that when they took up this detached attitude to their own story the moral was quite the reverse from that which medievalism had drawn. There had been setbacks and disasters but, on the whole, throughout history man had advanced to ever greater power. The crest of each wave of culture reached higher than the one before it. Nor was the advance purely in power. Man had shown that though he made many initial blunders he could learn to carry his new powers with increased responsibility. The dawn of the Great Societies such as the Empires of China and Rome had disclosed that there had been a growth of moral sense which accepted the new idea of the brotherhood of man. The belief and reliance upon Reason had also gone on. By the middle of the nineteenth century this triad of civilisation, Power, Humanitarianism and Reason, had certainly carried Western Europe to an unparalleled height. The man of that age had vision, resources and good will. The past to him looked like a victory, and the future like a triumph. These were the facts. How, then, might an author of discouragement hope to get a hearing?

There were three obvious reasons why a large minority might fail to appreciate their age's advance.

In the first place the new conditions were unfamiliar. Men resented new forms of hardship not because they were harder than the old ones, but because they were unaccustomed. They therefore tended to look back at the Past, which was innocent of such irking novelties, as an age of happiness. The medieval period began to be represented as an age of gold simply because it was pre-industrial. And undoubtedly the early modern age, partly because it was nearer true medievalism, partly because of a certain uncritical impatience with trammels, had dismissed medievalism too lightly. The belief in medievalism was bound, therefore, to return, with the added advantage that after another couple of centuries those relics which survived were naturally those which had either uncommon beauty or uncommon strength. The middens and the ramshackling had disappeared. The gaunt architecture stood out in skeleton severity which fancy clothed with the glowing colours it picked from the miniatures of the illuminators.

To this cause of discontent was added a second reason why the modern industrial age seemed inhumane and a collapse from a more socially minded culture. It was not only that the *theory* of medieval society was in advance of the *laissez-faire* of the nineteenth century and that the hopelessly inadequate *practice* of medievalism was yet to be proved by appeal to contemporary evidence. The immense growth in modern populations itself put an immensely increased strain on the social conventions inherited from a far smaller and more stable society. Much of the law ceased really to be applicable, and men had to think out again their relations with each other.

And there was yet a third cause of discontent, deeper and more effective, to blind men to the objective progress they had made. The ignorant, as we have seen, were unduly vexed by the unfamiliarity of their discomforts. All failed to allow for the real and great increase in social feeling, because none fully realised how much the increase in power and numbers required automatically an increase in good will and clear thinking, if even the moderate social standard of the pre-industrial world was to be maintained. And thirdly, the advanced reformers, because they were actuated by a heightened sense of sympathy, but were unable to appreciate this change in themselves, increasingly felt to be intolerable, social conditions which their ancestors would have accepted without protest. The ignorance of history, which is all too common among reformers, kept them unaware that a few generations before, men with as much public power as themselves and of as severe a private life, tolerated, sanctioned, and even enforced a legal code which, if to-day applied to an animal, would awaken general indignation.

We see, then, three reasons why Read's work met with a welcome. And if we go further and analyse them more deeply these three reasons help us to appreciate the importance of Read's position and its place in our historical advance. For, briefly, *The Martyrdom of Man* is a protest against the material optimism which was most amply advocated by Herbert Spencer. It is a protest which has to be in terms of its time, but a protest it is, and its success was due to the fact that it found many people who were discouraged and did not understand why they so felt, indeed were ashamed at their feeling and were looking for arguments with which to sustain it. These arguments had to run, in that age, in the form of an attack on spiritual tyranny, but the real force behind the attack sprang from a feeling of spiritual emptiness. Had Progress, as the nineteenth century conceived it, satisfied man, he would have left the past alone, or, if he thought of it, have quickly forgiven it. His sense of being wronged sprang from a sense of dislocation in himself. The new idea of Progress did nothing to solve that. It gave him a vast view of the past and the future, on which he could see humanity moving up, but his new sensibility and vision, which made possible that view, also made him realise that if that was all the truth, then all the past was simply a means to the present, and the present, in which alone he himself could live, was but a moment, and was a means to a future. Could he with such vision be content with such a conclusion? His sensibility refused to let him look upon all the past mankind as means to his moment; and the same sensibility made that moment, as far as he himself was privately concerned, look painfully inadequate. There was Progress; but, for a goal which no one could see, all the past and himself, the present, must be sacrificed. Both his selfishness and his altruism were left unsatisfied. As we can see from the last words of Read's book (when he speaks of the loss that man must suffer of the hope of immortality) it was this sense that psychological factors had been left out that inspired the author and gave him his public. Read's book is then significant because it is the forerunner of psychological history. His point of view was transitional. He was holding out, against too crude an optimism and too one-sided a notion of Progress, for the recognition of man as a whole. The way he put his case was itself too crude, but the force that made him put it was right. History is the history not of men, but of Man, but this Man is something other than simply the acts of all men. This being is linked and links men not merely through their deeds; he is not an abstraction, but a being that is æon by æon growing in reality and making it more and more possible for men to find their fulfilment in him. The life of men is vain unless this being lives. The recognition of Progress was right, but the idea itself had to undergo progress. Men had to recognise that Progress was incomplete, and indeed vain, unless it included progress in themselves, a growth of mind and consciousness equal to the growth of power and vision. So Read and Herbert Spencer can be reconciled. If we view all the achievements and discoveries that make up man's history as symptoms of the emergence of man, as steps in his discovery of himself; if we trace, as to-day we can trace, the growth of this sense that we are part of this being and really have our lives in it; men can be satisfied with the idea of Man going on; this can reconcile their vision of time and also their demand that they themselves shall not be dwarfed and made contemptible by their vision. So we can see Read's place in history, and so this sketch is put forward to show, if not how, at least where the side he spoke for and the side that Herbert Spencer represented may each, with its essentials recognised, meet and complement each other.

THE EMERGENCE OF MAN

NOTE

The following list gives the sources from which the material used in the head-pieces printed at the beginning of the chapters has been taken: –

Introduction. – The head of the Neanderthal Man is from a model by Guernsey Mitchell made to the instructions of Prof. H. A. Ward of Chicago and reproduced in *The Rise of Man* by Paul Carus (Chicago 1907).

Chap. 1. – Based on Algerian rock drawings as shown in Spearing's *Childhood of Art.*

Chap. 2. – As Chap. 1, 2nd Prehistoric Period.

Chap. 3. – Statue of 2nd Dynasty (Cairo Museum) reproduced in Spearing's *Childhood of Art.*

Chap. 4. – King Aknaton, from Wilkinson's *Ancient Egyptians* (1871).

Chap. 5. – King Assurnasirpal (884-860 B.C.) (British Museum).

Chap. 6. – Based on coins reproduced in Humphrey's *Coin Collectors Annual* (1880), showing Gold Stator of Colophon; Coin of Syracuse; Silver Coin of Lete; Silver Coin of Argos; Primitive Coin of Miletus; Silver Coin of Ceos.

Chap. 7. – Palace of Tiryns reproduced in Luckenbach's *Kunst und Geschichte* (1913).

Chap. 8. – Fragment from Temple of Agina.

Chap. 9. – Problem of Surfaces in Contact. Solid Geometry.

Chap. 10. – Inscription on a grave unearthed in the Appian Way. 'Know thyself.'

Chap. 11. – Banner of the Inquisition.

CHAPTER I

THE EMERGENCE OF THE HALF-MEN –
THE APE HORIZON

I

'FROM whomever you are descended, I am ascended from an ape.' This is the attitude of man to-day towards his past, and it is the fundamental basis of his optimism. The belief in progress, which sometimes overstates its claims, and so has a rude setback, has this immovable foundation. Progress may go more slowly and more deviously than we wish, but

B 17

the longer the view the surer is the conviction that man has progressed.

This optimism was impossible to the Greeks. They lacked the knowledge of past history necessary to establish it. In the nineteenth century, with the realisation of man's physical ascent from an ape-like creature, as we have seen, Herbert Spencer definitely maintained that, because of that physical evolution, Progress was a fact. Nevertheless, doubt remained in men's minds and the welcome given to the *Martyrdom of Man* showed that to many Progress had not proved its case. Something more was needed than the demonstration that man had been an ape to persuade him to-day that mankind was a success, that everything was going well and getting better. It was necessary to show that his powers had not outrun his capacities, and that the distress which he too often experienced when confronted with his actual achievement was significant and might be beneficial. What if his discontent should always outrun his efforts to assuage it? What became of the doctrine of Progress if all advance was really due to, and could only spring from, an intolerable irritation with present conditions?

A new conception of history was therefore required. The elder notion had been that man was born a free individual but, as Rousseau said, 'everywhere is he in chains.' Such a fancy was obviously what psychologists call a projection – a distressing condition which is really due to something in the

mind itself being imagined to be in the world outside, as sometimes people suffering from optical
disease see shapes they take to be external objects,
but which are really minute opacities in the lens of
the eye itself. So the past historians spoke of the
tyrannies of custom, of priestcraft, of kingly
authority, as though these things were objects
external to man, as though there had once been
a society of perfectly reasonable, fully self-conscious
individuals and that over these intelligent, kindly,
independent people, through some device as mysterious as the serpent's intrusion into Eden, the
magician, the priest and the king had suddenly
usurped power. So to think was to be as unscientific
as the sentimentalist who commiserated with the
oyster shut up in its shell. We can now fortunately
write an account of history less self-centred, more
hopeful and more reasonable than this; less self-
centred because the past can be interpreted more
objectively. So previous mankind can be seen not
simply as ourselves denied our comforts, but different in tastes and even in apprehensions, as it was
different in circumstances; more hopeful because
that same discovery, that man's spirit evolves,
suggests not only that in the main he is more com-
placent than he cared to confess toward his present
circumstances, but that, as he is largely their maker,
he may extricate himself from his present discontents as soon as he is resolved really to do so; more
reasonable because this psychical extension of the

idea of evolution not only shows how man may extricate himself, but also explains why he fell into the present discontents and why they are to-day become so acute.

The story that follows is therefore an attempt to tell briefly man's career from the earliest times until to-day. Such a sketch must be summary, tentative, temerarious. Its justification is that it attempts to keep a balance, and while accepting all that man has done as part of man's deliberate achievement (religion as much as science and war as much as law) to see each stage and each device not as the attainment of a good, but as a rudiment. All man's work is an effort to express a need. But the work does not necessarily relieve the need. For the moment some form, be it military success, religious systematisation or philosophic speculation, may have assuaged the inner appetite. It could not permanently satisfy it. For, in the first place, that inner demand was not a self-conscious desire; it was not a demand which could be clearly set out and therefore clearly met. It was a vague discontent, restlessness, a sense of thwarting, an exasperated realisation of futility.

The consequences which such a state brings about cannot be satisfying for they are not purposive, intentional, a clear realisation of what is lacking and so a clear conception of how that lack may be filled. Rather the actions of men who lack self-knowledge must be like the actions of an irritated animal. Men can only strike out using reflexes. The ends so achieved are nothing, and the emotional satisfaction given by the action must be inadequate. In the second place the inner desire itself must grow as it learns to know itself. It will demand not only exacter but wider satisfaction.

This, then, is the line that will be followed. History is, *au fond*, the history of man finding himself. All his physical achievement, constructive or destructive, can be co-ordinated, and only so, if we view it as the symptom of his realisation, first of what he really needs, and then of what he is, what he has been and what he may be. That, it seems, is the great contribution which the advance in psychology has been able to make toward the study of history. It is a contribution so great that it is, this writer believes, bringing about a revolution in the study and interpretation of the past. For now it seems growing constantly more clear that man only acts, and even apprehends, according to the stage and degree of his mental emergence. The sympathy expended upon the past, the sense that it was a Tragedy and a Martyrdom, the gallant wish to put ourselves in their place, all these emotions, however creditable and natural to the nineteenth century, can now be seen to have been mistaken. This attitude may have been philanthropic, it was not historical. The philanthropic, complex. counter-controlled society of to-day which the men of to-day are mainly agreed is, if not the final state of civilisation, at least the latest step toward that goal, that society would have been as alien, distasteful and even impossible to the men of the past as their social forms are repugnant to us. For the truth, psychology makes clear to us, is that it is the mind of man that deposits the social form in which man lives. As a great craniologist has said, it is the brain that makes the skull, not the skull that shapes the brain. Naturally we fully individualised constituents of a modern individualised State viewed with horror the indifference to individuality and its 'rights' which we see in earlier societies. We also viewed with contemptuous pity the absurd value the men of those states and that day placed upon their union with the State. We commiserated with their physical sufferings, but lost patience when we discovered how often and how easily they could have freed themselves had they not been tied by a superstitious devotion to the community and an absurd dread of daring to live apart from it. Now we realise that this setting psychical pleasure and pain above physical pleasure and pain was as natural in the past as the reverse is obvious to-day. For the reason is plain: Man was not individualised as we are. The unit of humanity was not the physical individual, and so the physical feelings of that individual were not decisive. The unit was the society, group, horde or nation – and when it acted, then all its constituents were united and mixed in it, as are the cells and leucocytes in the body, though individual, united and moved by the unity and direction of the undivided organism. In such a society the constituents are so tied together that it is easier for them to endure the severest attacks on their persons than to loose their ties.

What we now can see in history, the clue to the entire sequence and process is, then, this: The Emergence of Man. All his acts and achievements, however extravagant and even contradictory they must appear when only viewed by themselves, can be co-ordinated and understood if we realise that they are shadows cast on the outer world by the changing shape of his spirit, projections and symptoms of a slow inner evolution of the mind whereby it has stage by stage taken on its present form. As in the palæontological record of the rocks we have learnt to recognise as stages toward our present form, types which, till the idea of evolution was grasped, were thought wholly distinct, so now we can see the stable 'superstitious,' Magical æon, the Heroic Age of violent strife, and our present individualised Scientific Age as all connected, successive, inevitable phases of a single evolutionary process – evolution[1] being carried on now in the mind as it was once carried on in the body. Each stage, therefore, of this mental evolution apprehended as much of the outer world as it could assimilate, and with that apprehension precipitated

[1] Note also that in this phase of evolution Natural Selection is also still working, but, as evolution is now mental or psychic, so also is Natural Selection; and see later, p. 124.

the social form that answered the apprehension and expressed the mental evolutionary stage that man had reached.

The sketch of history that follows is based on this underlying plan. It will be obvious that following this plan necessitates two profound modifications of the usual outline of history. In the first place history must give pride of place to prehistory. All the decisions that ruled that man should be man were taken in the prehistoric æon. We must therefore begin by attempting to show man at his most formative stage, at that decisive stage when his unit the Group was so building itself up that it and he might cease to be animal and that, finally, from that shell should be released man as we know him to-day in ourselves, man the critically minded, scientifically hypothesising individual.

In the second place in this sketch of history and prehistory the incidents and illustrative detail must be different from the standard examples. In what must be called pre-psychological history the incidents were, first, battles; then political developments, treaties and constitutions; next economic movements, agriculture, trade, commerce, population and, lastly, cultural evolution, the emergence and diffusion of ideas, discovery, invention. This shift of interest shows a tendency toward the proince of psychology. But once that province is entered we must be prepared greatly to modify the whole presentation. For psychology has made clear two principles which must alter the whole 'scale of importance.' The first is the principle that what is really significant in any phase is not the manifest but the latent; that those events which seem decisive and characteristic of an age are really already spent. 'Nothing fails like success,' the Dean of St. Paul's profound epigram is recognition of this fact; that whatever is fully expressed is already over — for the concrete event is only a symptom and projection of a mental condition, and once the condition has uttered itself it is delivered, changed, and begins to shape quite another expression to convoy its changed nature. Therefore we must in this outline bring out those details and incidents which are, though small in actual size, yet crescent, and when the incident swells to an economic or political event then we must abandon it — its further development, however big it loom in the material world, is really a decadence. The second principle follows from the first. It is, that great significance lies not only in customs and activities which have yet to become of economic and political magnitude, but in many practices which will never do so. Psychology teaches us to watch carefully for and to trace symptoms which may in themselves be very small, but which may be of immense significance because they indicate how man's spirit is evolving, how he is becoming aware of himself, and of his relationship with his situation. In obeying the first principle much therefore will be omitted from this sketch that finds pride of place in former outlines; in obeying the second much will be noted that the former outlines dismissed as trivial.

The lines are now clear. We can proceed on them.

II

Till now history has seemed tragic because it was conceived too materialistically. The pre-psychological historian who had yet to apply the idea of evolution to the mind as well as to the body – the further his view was extended backward the more he could only see men increasingly up against conditions of such severity that he could not imagine them having any time for aught but physical considerations. All that was left for his inspection was their sorry gear, and this provoked the subjective assumption that their only concern can have been a definite conscious struggle to satisfy appetite – a concentration on means. As we had only their material means we were bound to construct their motives by putting ourselves in their place. But this we see was little less mistaken than the misplaced pity with which an untrained naturalist watches the restless vigilance of a worm-eating thrush. Certainly the reading of a modern man's mentality into primitive man's condition has not given us a satisfactory history.

Let us therefore, as was done in geometry in the

nineteenth century, with such fruitful results, for a moment make other assumptions and see whether, using these, the facts do not yield a more comprehensible picture. And when we deal with really primitive man, our stock stripped till it is as naked of culture as an ape, there is another – an outer – reason for revising our assumptions as to its wretchedness. For not only was this creature careless, without regrets or apprehensions, as no fully conscious human being can be. The conditions under which it lived were genial. The ape man is not glacial man. Probably it was the cold that tempered him into cultural manhood; all the time he was preparing for that test he was probably not up against a climate even as hard as ours. The struggle to exist was not his pressing concern. He may well have been a food-gatherer as are the great apes of to-day, or the South Sea Islanders, and have sauntered through existence much as do they. Certainly 'no hungry generations trod him down.' All change was on such a gentle and vast scale that no individual ever felt its outer pressure or inner urge.

We may, then, take as the datum line when man rose above the ape the stage at which he descended from the tree. Conditions had so far favoured him, and his innate capacities had so far responded, that he had grown in bulk. The tiny tarsier can crouch in the modern human hand. The loris can be held on the wrist. The largest surviving lemur on the arm. The gibbon and chimpanzee on the

shoulder. But Pithecanthropus, Eoanthropus and
Sinanthropus – the fossil 'trial men' – are of the
stature of small men of to-day. They were too heavy
for the branches, a fall was too serious. So Nature
finally furled their tails and, as they were large
enough to look after themselves on the ground,
launched them from the leafy stocks, where they
had been built up, to set out on their annexation of
the earth. Man is arboreal, but not confirmedly so.
His early anatomy and attitudes show that he had
a tree penchant once. But as soon as he was predominantly human, the tree became his base rather
than his bound. So the picture that follows shows
him already to have chosen parkland as preferable
to jungle. It also shows the apes evolving too. They
go on, but toward the dead end of specialisation.
Clinging to the forest, they have become parasitic
on it, and the chimpanzee, the gibbon and the orang
have tended to become hook-handed. So a picture
of this date must show the issue between the ape
stocks still undecided. The Life Force has long
decided that Intelligence shall lead. That decision
means that flexibility and mobility shall always win
against strength and stability. The crown of life is
therefore now in the ape family. But which branch of
them should rule? Many were in the line of succession, many could claim to inherit the only real
blood royal, the blood that builds a larger brain.
The royal lines were many because the succession
was still open.

THE EMERGENCE OF THE HALF-MEN

Geologically speaking – and we may so speak at this age because it must be repeated animal man is geological man, and animal man, because he has no conception of his individual life, is timeless – geologically speaking, it had but lately been decided that brain should be the one claim to power. Muscle was still in the running. Through cunning the apes could decline battle with the lords of wood and field and sometimes they could outwit them in actual conflict, but to look them in the face and dispute their supremacy, that was yet to happen. So, many varieties of brains are being produced. Dryopithecus and Sivapithecus are two types of super-apes produced at this time. Though to-day they have been long extinct they had brains equal to, and maybe surpassing, those of any surviving ape. Such brains can only be looked on as experimental. They did not take the brunt. Before they could be brought into action the creatures in which they developed had been defeated and gone under. These super-apes became extinct before they could raise themselves above animal level.

The next step is man. But that step is not into full manhood, but only into trial manhood. Now, however, we can presume that the brain really began to tell, and it is therefore at this level that we must attempt to get our first picture of man's history.

III

The climate is on the whole mild, and when the winter comes it is little more than tonic. Life is happy enough. The parkland stretches for these simple folk to the world's end. The world's centre is this noble Tree. The sun rises on that primal human day, and round the Tree's base the males – who have slept huddled in the lowest crutches of its span, stretch themselves, yawn, clamber down and call. Immediately above in the branches a score of cries reply. All sorts of sounds are bandied. The squealing and shouting takes on the rhythm of a simple chorus. Those on the ground interrogate. Those up aloft answer. It is like an orchestra tuning up. It is indeed. It is the great orchestra of human speech being practised and its technique mastered against those works which, æons after, are to be composed. Now the pack is shouting, laughing and yodelling from pure virtuosity. It is a delight to hum and howl, running up and down the scale, as the friendly stimulating voices of all the others blend, diverge, glance on an unexpected harmony and break into happy pandemonium. The group's activity increases. Arms and legs swing to the noise. A junior suddenly swings right out of the Tree plumb into the middle of the chanting, swaying elders below. There is a dart of hands, but off he goes round the great bole with squeals of apprehensive challenge. The Tree rains its living fruit.

The pack gambols round its sanctuary. They wrestle, they roll, they chant. Voice and limb are wreathed. The rhythmic game, like a current, tumbles them. They are bathed and refreshed in the group gymnastic. Suddenly from the brake, not farther than the great tree's shadow stretches just before sleep, there is a sound . . . not loud, but none the better for that. Out of the merry commotion of the maypole dance raises himself the bravest male. The rest remain stilled, looking at him and then swinging eyes toward where he stares. His nose is thrust out. His foot rises; he stamps. He is shaken with anger that the fun should be broken in upon. 'Ugh!' he cries. 'Ugh!' The hatred and disgust in his voice electrifies his hearers. He is brave and defiant, but, through his tone, they realise the horror he is diagnosing. He barks out his defiance again against the mysterious bush, and at that all save his closest pals swarm up into the branches. Warily he watches their retreat, all the while keeping his face to the danger. They did not take to the Tree empty-handed. Each as he swung to safety held a stone in his mouth or fist. The last up, with a snort the hero and his comrades also follow. The Tree becomes as still as though deserted. Then the bush moved and into the dappled sunlight came out, sniffing the air, a full-grown lion. Cat-like his nose dipped to the ground as he padded up to the Tree. There about the roots he drew long breaths. Appetite blazed. He lifted his head to the branches, stirred his great loins uneasily, and the sense of bafflement broke from him in a roar. The roar galvanised the tree. It broke into a frenzy of counter abuse. The lion roared contemptuously back, but suddenly his contemptuous anger was shot with pain. One of the great fangs thrown exposed was struck and broken. Before he could wince, a second stone struck sharply and deep, cutting open his left eyeball. Stones drummed on snout, on ears, on skull, on loins. Half blinded, in keen pain, a new sensation took the beast — Fear. What was in the Tree that struck so swiftly and so hard and yet was not in his claws' reach? With a bound he was clear of the Tree's baleful purlieus. He stood by the brake looking with what vision he still had at the looming object, sniffing with bruised snout that peculiar smell. Food, no doubt, but somehow ill food. He shrunk away, licking the blood that trickled in his mouth, blinking the eye that no longer saw.

A shout broke from the Tree. A moment after the maypole ring re-formed. Round the great bole they gambolled. A piece of creeper hung around the brave one's neck. As it shifted, hands replaced it. He coiled it himself. They all noticed it. Stones, the good stones, were passed from hand to hand, were licked, mouthed and cuddled. The dear Tree, it, too, was caressed. Tower of strength. How it uplifted and protected. Was it not theirs, was it not greater than everything else? The exultation began to slacken. Why, no one had had anything yet to eat. One of the brave ones stood up, stone in hand, others joined him. Off they went over the open heath – giving wide berth to thickets. The sun was up above now and the Tree's shade pleasant for those that kept home. Every now and then one would run down to the pool that glittered and take his drink and so back to the Tree, there to play and groom and exercise, to wrestle and yodel and wreathe the creepers into knots and plaits. Yes, life was good. The group was healthy. Three nights ago an old one had slipped and fallen out of the Tree. The next morning it was still at the foot dragging a broken leg and whimpering. As they looked down on it, suddenly they felt it had become something disgusting, hostile. Someone ran to the deep cleft where a store of stones was always heaped and, picking one, flung it at the monster. As the stone struck, it yelped. At once half a dozen more struck it. It broke away stumbling toward the bush. The rest howled their excommunication at it. The next day as they hunted they came on scraps of its carcase. A lion had eaten it. But looking at it they no longer felt disgust or even interest. Would the Tree feel love, interest or disgust as it looked down on the leaves it had shed?

IV

For that reason it was not long before the next age dawned for the trial men, the next test of their power to endure change. Years must be told off by the hundreds of thousands if this æon is to be checked by years. But years had yet to come into man's consciousness. He will have to go timelessly and with the speed of timelessness through many changes yet, before his consciousness will have condensed and focused even enough to conceive of moons. He has yet to reach the month, and beyond that he must stretch his apprehension twelve times before he can conceive the year. That strange problem of time; of how the creatures with the shortest time sense, to whom each day is an æon, the ephemeræ, approach eternity; of how when each moment is inarticulated with the next, each separate glimpse of consciousness is completely static and so is as eternal as an instantaneous snapshot; of how, as consciousness extends, we grow even more conscious of the shortness of *our* time; that problem must, as we have seen, follow us throughout this sketch of history and will set its *tempo*. For the discovery of time is the discovery of our age, and it has made all past history need rewriting in its light. No other age could conceive how relative time really is. And yet if it is relative, as we believe, then there is no study that is more affected by its relativity than is history. Take a

34

simile from space. The mile was made by travelling
man as his outdoor standard. It was the largest
convenient group of smaller spans – one thousand
paces. Nor did the horse much over-strain it.
But when it was used as an abstract standard, it
was shown at once to be too home-made. Astronomy
made it ridiculous and so mileage is no longer used
for the star distances, any more than a liner's
voyage would be calculated in millimetres. The
'light-year' now is the scale of inter-stellar space,
and already it is being strained. So with time 'there
was a time when time was not.' When consciousness was not continuous in the individual animal
then each day was an æon, an eternity. The sun
that rose would not be the sun that set, but belong
to another life, another creation. We can understand how this was if we recall our own individual
earliest childhood. How slower and slower goes
time as we trace back our memory to its source.
And yet, astronomically, the weeks and months
and years all through our lives and the lives of men
have been going as to-day they go. And the longer
we live the quicker time flies. These obvious plati-
tudes become illuminating when we consider them
under our new conception of time, as something
predominantly in us. For when we were children
our own change was so rapid that we ourselves were
different beings each year. Further back we were
different beings each month. Finally we reach such
a speed of change that the sense of continuity is no

longer possible. We are abreast of time. We are eternal because we change as fast as any sense we have of outer change. But it may be said this is not eternity. This is extinction. Time is overcome by the simple solution of dissolving the creature that could experience time. Is that so? Look at the facts. There is no dissolution. The child is a growing, highly co-ordinated creature. It has character and motive at one and two, and yet it will have no memory of this stage, nor at that time has it a sense of time, of life hurrying by, of a self which must be guarded against change. Its growth is being directed more perfectly, with a complete abandonment of the outgrown and a complete assumption of the new, than it will ever after be able to achieve. It is a dynamic unity as, when self-consciousness appears, it must cease to be. It and Time are in step. The life which directs it and which is interfered with by the growth of a separate self-conscious individuality, that life has the true *tempo*, it neither looks before or after, nor sighs for what is not, it is eternal. So was it with the trial men. As individuals they did not have to make any more effort than the leaves have to make an effort to serve the Tree; as individuals they did not exist any more than the leaves of the Tree. That solves the problem of time in their respect. But that is not to say there was no consciousness, no intention or direction. That would be to deny the facts even more than to say that they individually directed

36

the current of their lives. There was consciousness, but it resided not in the individual but in the species. Here lay the power of change and by the scale of generic and speci-al change can we gauge the *tempo* of that elder consciousness. The scale we use at this date must not be that of the rapid reproductive cycle of generations, but the vast scale on which the divisions are marked by the evolutionary modifications of physical characteristics. This is a difficult concept even now for us. But the time has come that, as we have to conceive of several sorts of times, so we must take the next step and see that this is so because there are several forms or qualities of consciousness. Until this generation we conceived of reality as something made of two distinct parts, of dead matter and self-consciousness individuals, and we caulked any awkward gaps between with the word Instinct. But now we see we have to conceive of a scale of consciousness not less extensive and elaborate than the scale of physical forms. So we see the martyrdom of man is largely an anthropomorphism. That concept of a self-conscious individual struggling against his tyrants is a concept from our own age read into one in which it really has no meaning. So we can pass generations during which the trial men themselves are the artefacts out of which the racial consciousness, which is handed on in the rapid repetition of the procreative cycle, is shaping the intenser form that is to be. The life of humanity, its inventive power and quickening purpose, is at this level not in the single individual, nor in the single generation any more than the action of a film is in any of its innumerable 'stills.'

V

So as we watch, there still stands the great Tree, centre, shelter and support of the group's life, armature around which this the first society is sustained. But, should we slow down our cinematograph projector to a speed which no longer shows man growing as a species, we should see that the tree is in detail not the same tree. Sometimes we see it is an oak, sometimes a sycamore, sometimes a beech. Go still slower, the oak is that same oak that we first saw. Twenty such had risen and fallen since the sub-human group loved its tree. Suns flicker past as sunlight dapples on a forest floor. Seasons, as cloud shadows in April, chase across the downs. One day, as the group sat about its bole, its nostrils full of rich safe scents, a tang struck one nose as to-day a live wire can sting an unwary hand. The hunting had been good. For the trial men had managed to obey life and eat as widely as might be. They had eaten well of a large gathering of roots and berries and succulent fungus, but from their sharp teeth they were picking fragments of flesh, the children were still gnawing small bones and the mothers were giggling as they placed fragments of pelt sometimes on their heads or on their necks. Æons before, the rabbit that bolted from under the ape man's foot was snatched up and killed in a moment. The hawk and the jackal ate with relish. The ape man tasted. It was tasty, the warm flesh, and it was invigorating. They that ate animals thrived, so the half-men all sat round the bole in vigorous calm. Then came again that tang. One cried out at the shock of it. At once all, even those who had not been struck, howled with horror. Then the sharp one, he who used both to smell and also to look, he pointed and in a moment they all saw as clearly as he, that face looking at them. It wasn't panic they felt. This was no roarer or render. This was something simply unnatural. People didn't rush into the Tree. Rather they stood looking at it with a fascinated disgust. In the silence a young one suddenly vomited. With a bound the leaders were after the thing. It shambled off, but they were too fast for it. The Dryopithecus was surrounded. It showed its teeth and roared its desperate defiance. They closed in on it like inquisitors on an unnatural sinner. Someone flung a stone that, hitting the beast on the neck as it drew itself up, disturbed its balance. At once they were on it. Twice it bit hard but clumsily. They left it the moment it was still, walking slowly off and now and then looking back. Before night and the hyenas came, the men of the Tree heard a whimper and saw reddish forms mopping and moving where they had left the body. Every one snarled, but stayed by the Tree. The red forms disappeared soon. After that no one again saw a great ape. The fear of the cunning fury of the Tree-men had spread and the apes gave them wider and wider berth, letting their best feeding-grounds be trespassed and annexed and going off lamely to seek others.

The next incident was graver. Again that tang of smell; again the sense of something unnatural, but this time not one shape but several. The Tree group gathered itself to launch against the intrusion but hesitated. As it delayed, out into the full sunlight rolled an unbelievable creature. One of themselves, but, no, it couldn't be. It was horribly close, a forgery on their confidence and sense of right. And the effrontery to come in this way toward their Tree! The confused feelings became organised into steady anger. And then the one became several. They stood looking steadfastly at the Tree. No one made a sound. Then, without a sign, they wheeled and ambled off. The Tree's people followed, at a safe distance. Every now and then the intruders stopped and looked back. Then stopped the Tree's people. Finally when the Tree was getting unpleasantly far away, one of its people flung a stone at the strangers. It went well, striking a laggard on the nape. He howled and ran up to the rest and they, catching his pain and fear, swung off. The Tree's men began running, too, till one of the intruders turned and himself flung clumsily a small stone. As it bounded toward the Tree-men they stopped and looked at it; one bent and smelt its horrid smell with misgiving. The pull of the Tree became stronger. The Tree group recoiled back into it.

Several such passes between the other trial men took place. Every few centuries one type overflowed into the country of another type. The boundaries fluctuated, for already they had boundaries. Their life focused round the Tree, but beyond that spot light or *fovea* there was a circle of country-side – their country, known and lived upon and in which they felt a peculiar concern. But the raids of other species of man were rare and grew rarer. That did not, however, mean that the Tree fell into fat lethargy. The slinking snarlers were less troublesome. More and more they gave way. They recognised this odd being was food, but a more dangerous food than any other. He stung at a distance, farther than a spring, and he was pertinacious, a creature like a giant swarm of hornets. Better give him a wide berth. Spring on a laggard if you could, but his Tree – that was dangerous ground. So the young had fewer nightmares. Those green slit eyes suddenly aglare, level with you on the branch – that was a horror less and less often stamped into mind. But the snakes were stupider than the cats and learnt more slowly that the young of the Tree-men were costlier prey than the young of the monkeys. So, still, the young knew, too often to forget, the sudden coming to life of a

small branch, its hiss, the stroke and the helpless
fall. Fewer and fewer dreamed of cats and shud-
dered at their smell, but still many in the night
howled because of a swift rustle, awoke screaming
and clutching their mothers because the safe Tree
seemed to have let them drop into the gulf below.
Yet fat lethargy would have come had not success
brought its own problems. The Tree people's
prosperity overloaded the Tree. The pressure
made random gambollings become savage squabbles.
Sides were taken – the single-celled society was
about to divide. One day after a savage brawl, as
they drew apart, three of them lay dead. The
stronger group had held near to the Tree. The
smaller looked across the dead at those already
clambering up into the branches. Suddenly the
Tree seemed alien. One or two whimpered, one
actually touched a corpse that lay near and moaned.
Then one of the stronger who had fought fiercely,
shouted, shook his arm at the Tree. The rest
gathered round him. He threw a stone at the Tree.
It hit the trunk and bounded among the roots.
The Tree was silent. It was not their Tree, they
became sure. The leader wheeled and they followed.
Now the Tree seemed something to get away from.
They went on till everything they associated with it
was gone. They went out of its country till they
saw no more any landmark that they knew. Then
as the dusk came on they smelt for water and
found a stream. They drank, gathered food, and that

night slept on a ledge half-way up a rocky bluff against which the stream bent. The next day they went on their march until about noon they saw a Tree like their Tree, yet other, there, standing up to welcome them. They came home to it with a sense of return and yet renewal. How friendly, how ample, how much for them it was.

So diffusion continued. Sometimes there were throwbacks. One Tree, as it were, fell back into the orbit of another Tree, frontiers were infringed and there was random fighting, but on the whole the urge was centrifugal. It was grand to find a new Tree to claim as one's own when the old Tree had grown unfriendly. So must Archanthropos have pushed out, and before him moved away Pithecanthropos, Eoanthropos, and the others. He did not exterminate them. Nature is no narrow rationalist; she does not push things to conclusions. In chess it is not necessary to take many pieces to win the game. In Natural Selection one species of wild animals forces out another, not by direct action but by indirect pressure. The marsupial wolf, that now hangs on in Tasmania, once was spread over Australia. Then down came from the north the mammal wild dog, the dingo. Two types each suited to the same life could not last side by side. The more efficient took the land; needing the same food, the dog found it more efficiently, reared its young better, and the less efficient passed away. So with the trial men. As Archanthropos spread, the other sub-men gave way before him, left him their choice lands in which they had thriven, withdrew to poor districts and misery spots where they pined and finally died out.

VI

Then in the summer climate a cloud appeared that did not go away. The slow exposure camera (which we are using on this tract of history so as to record only the permanent changes) begins to show the Tree less creeper hung, the Tree itself more gaunt and the pool has a glaze on it, only a hint of ripple. The brown-green of the ground is greyer as into the web of the days more and more snow-white ones are blended. Then, as grey becomes the dominant colour, the fun goes out of life. The Earth is hard, vegetation spare and stringy, animals savage and scarce. The apes and the last of the ape men lumber off. They find gradually that things are still easy in one direction. They gravitate south. Eden is re-won. There the trees are more bountiful than ever. True, the ground is even more dangerous, and so they hang more and more up in the branches. The hand that was opening to grasp the world, and to untie its close-wound knots, shrinks again. Only one thing is required of it – not every possible thing. For a happy quiet life it can best serve by becoming a hook, and so the hands of the apes have become increasingly more hook-like than they were.

The ape has retreated geographically, and that retreat was confirmed by a physical decline. Then it was that Archanthropos stood his ground. The apes fell from being of Life's blood royal. The men-like alone were left. This bleak world was ceded to them and they chose to take it. That bluff where the river turned – in its rocks were deep clefts. It looked south. At midday a little sun made the shelf a place pleasant to lie in and at night when the stream underneath was silent in frost, the first cave-men crowded into the clefts with pieces of pelt over the shoulders and round the feet. All packed together, it was possible to doze in some comfort and safety. The snakes had gone with the ape. Only large animals now remained to threaten and they could not get into those crannies. The stone of the cleft was soft; as you scratched at it it came away. Sometimes you scooped out a bit which had pushed into your back as you were crowded up against the wall. Yet the wall was queer, for suddenly from being soft and white it became just for a spot, darker and very hard. You could wriggle your finger round the hard bit and then suddenly it would plop down on to the ground near you, sitting there, looking at you like a toad. You couldn't help poking at it with your foot, but it didn't stir. You had to push it harder before it would move. So it was picked up and hit against the wall. How it liked that. It bit into the soft wall far better than any finger-nail. Great mouthfuls came away. It was fun. And then it met another toad also buried in the wall. Crack it went against it. It would dig out its companion. Bump, bump it went and the chalk flew. Then crack, it hit its fellow again. It was dark in the cleft. Even outside it was a dreary thing to call a day. But surely the other stone had spoken to his fellow. Another blow and a spark flew. The wielder dropped his nodule. That was not right; that was bad. Had the others seen? No, they were huddled by the entrance, some gnawing, some grooming, all looking out at the valley. The scooper lolloped off and sat with them. But every now and then he looked back at the nodule lying quiet on the floor. Yes, it knew something. Then he forgot. Till one night he was pushed to the same corner. The half-freed nodule pushed him on the back. He began to pull at it. It came away in his hand. The others grunted and jostled him to keep quiet. He fell to sleep with it in his lap. In the morning it was warm and familiar, and how well it came to his hand. He hit the cave side. The nodule cut it like mud. He took it to the entrance. He noticed other nodules just sticking out round the cave's rim. He had never noticed them before. He hit one and it rolled out and down the bluff. In the light he saw no spark. But it had been angry. When he looked at his nodule's end a corner had been bitten off. It was black inside. It had a faint smell. He licked the smooth black piece, then dropped it angrily. It had bitten

46

him. His tongue was cut. He drew away and the others stopped watching, but he still kept on coming back to it – every time he felt his sore tongue. Finally he again touched the nodule gingerly. It did not bite him. He raised it. It fitted his hand as well as ever. He swung it and the end came down on a bit of root that here thrust across the cave's threshold. He thought the stone would bump back as sticks often did when you drummed on that bit of root. It didn't, and when he looked there was a deep clean bite in the tough root. The nodule had bitten it. So, with many lapses of forgetfulness they learned to make two nodules bite each other and then they would bite roots and sinews and bones. Biting stones became things the tribe tended to make. They sang as they struck the flints together. But mostly you struck them in the open. If you struck them in the dark of the caves they looked at you just for a moment as though they were going to do something worse even than bite you. At times they did bite, they bounded up and struck you. Then you left that one alone and worked with kind ones. When they grew tired of biting, you could make them get back their bite by setting them again to bite each other. Some people had pet stones – they fitted their hands so well that they would make them recover their bite again and again. But other people felt this wasn't right. Certainly if you went on trying to make a nodule bite better and better, sooner or later it

gleamed at you, and that of course was wrong.
Every one felt sure of that, and one day it was
proved. One who loved his nodule very much – it
was a very fine one – was making it get back its bite.
He was very cunning. He could make the other
nodule only take away a tiny flake and yet after
that there was the bite sharper than ever. He was
doing this in the cave's mouth at the end of a fine
hot day in autumn. The cave mouth was deep
with whittlings from sticks other people had shar-
pened with their biting stones, feathers and down
plucked from birds' bodies, tufts of hair from pelts
and leaves and bracken which had been dragged
here, to lie on in the sun. Several were watching,
but no one saw the stone get angry. It must have
sparked, but the first thing people knew was that
the hot horror was actually in the middle of them.
They saw his signal, the blue thread that can't be
handled and yet which smells so rank. Then
someone saw himself very small and red moving
among the bracken bedding. With a crackle he
sprang up. In panic the group rushed into the cave.
The flame stood up in front of the opening. They
could feel its hot breath. Once it bowed and
seemed as though it was going to come in after
them. They barked with terror as its choking horror
swept in round them. But, a moment after, it flew
back, standing again straight up. For a lifetime
they seemed to be cowering in front of the fury,
until at last the strain was too great. They sat still

in coma. Then one at the back began to groom the shoulder nearest him. The terror lifted and they saw the flame had sunk. The sun also had set. So the burnt bedding glowed in the dusk. Then with a shift, and a cataract of sparks, part of the emberage fell down the bluff. In a few moments it was possible to steal out of the cave warily, keeping face to the remaining glow. With the sunset had come the frost. It was too cold to stay out. They crept back into the cave, and there it was as though the sun was still up. They sat in the glow first silently, then chattering with pleasure. In the cool part of the ashes someone picking about found roast acorns, another a big bone split with heat. Both had an added flavour. As the glow died they crept toward it. They did not want this kindly warm thing to disappear. When they woke it was, however, gone. No one could call it back, but also no one remembered to be vexed with the sharpener. No one knew he had made fire. They had forgotten how the fire came, because from horror it had turned to comfort. Neither he nor a long line of succeeding flakers struck fire again, but the sparks no longer frightened men. Then again tinder caught. Fire was found and lost many times. At last it stayed. The flint had brought first the power to cut and shape and pierce, and then fire.

And not too soon, for still the cold grew, still the great glaciers creaked and groaned forward, gouging out the valleys, heaping their moraines on either sides. The beasts that stayed grew more savage. The cave bear standing twice a man's height no more feared flint-armed man than a coal-heaver fears an urchin armed with a chestnut. But a pack of humans armed with hot brands was a serious matter. He wanted their cave for his lair, their bodies for meat, but when they sat with that sentinel at the door he slunk off. Even when he was ensconced, fire would make it possible for them to drive him out. Its smoke blinded and choked him, and when he rushed out, sharp poles with glowing points struck him in eyes and nostrils, till panic-stricken, he broke from his victors a beaten monster. So their courage grew. They learned how to drive him till he fell over the bluff, his great bulk striking the rocks below, and as he lay maimed, they hurled rocks at him till one split his huge skull and he lay inert while flint choppers and knives dug him to pieces. The bear conquered, it was but a step to conquer the mammoth. When this earth-shaking beast fell down the slope men feasted till the valley stank. Then they thought of driving some laggard of the herd into a swamp. One had been found bogged and there beaten to death. The little morass was cleared and lightly covered. It became the first elephant trap.

VII

Meanwhile, the last of the trial men had fallen out. The Neanderthal had come so far. He had

found how to use fire. He had taken to caves and
endured part of the awful Ice Age. He had carried
on the craft of stone weapon-making until at one
stroke the flint yielded straight away an edged knife
which only needed finishing. The flint was now
part of his life and the dead, when put away, had
their flints put with them, for were these not as
their hands and teeth? Was it wholly safe to use
what had been their members? But Neanderthal
was too conservative. He clung to his vegetarian
diet. Fruit and roots were scarce. Man in an arctic
climate must be a carnivore or disappear. So Life
chose *Homo Sapiens*, subtle, adaptable, fierce and
curious, patient and clubable, a creature of mer-
curial energy, capable of passionate attachment
and resentment. He struck out that icy ordeal. It
left its mark on him. Such a hammering made him
harder. He had beaten into him virtues so hard
that they had in them a high alloy of vice. He was
a fiercer creature than before, more resourceful too,
and yet the group had been so hammered that in
spite of the units' greater cunning, they were no
more differentiated from it than were the sub-men
from their pack in the far distant Genial Age. But
these later packs showed their advance by an
intenser aggressiveness against all that came from
without. Yet the energy he generated to stand
against the cold did not discharge wholly in violence.
Those long dark hours in the cave began to be lit
by imagination. As the firelight flickered on the

walls he saw, in the irregularities of the surface,
glimmer out at him his brooding fancies. The most
fertile-minded saw most clearly. 'Don't you see the
bison's snout just there? I see it clearly. Look, I'll
point out where it is.' As he pointed they saw,
but when he ceased to show where the shadows had
helped out his fancy, for them the bison vanished.
'Make it again,' they cried. He took a piece of
charcoal-tipped stick. In the morning there was the
bison's head. The next day a bison was drawn to
the trap and killed. The picture had power. Who
could doubt it? The best hunters before setting out
asked the draughtsman, 'Have you seen bison
to-day?' 'Yes, in my mind I have them.' Then he
would draw over again the head. It was alive under
his hand. He had power to make it obey. Someone
drew a spear in its side. 'Good, good,' they shouted.
'Good hunting to-morrow.' Soon they saw bison
and deer in every jut and contour of the cave, and
large felines and the boar. Soon such skill had the
draughtsman that he no longer needed the jut of
the cave wall to give him his theme. He passed
from that dream stage when we take the bed curtain
for a visitant and then, waking, cannot even see why
its fold should have suggested a figure. He only
asked a fair surface and on it he could set down each
flow of the animal's outline. On bone and ivory he
etched them. And as his interest grew he noticed
and recorded fishes and birds. So by his game he
was drawn into a larger world. As he lay in the

cave mouth and drew that great folding line of the buffalo's front, the whirring of a grasshopper tickled his attention. There it sat grinding its legs. He snatched at it and it bounded. More wary, next time, he caught it clean and crunched it. It was pleasant. So he came to sketch this, too, the hors d'œuvre of his great meat repasts.

And as the artist grew in skill so his authority rose. Must he recreate, every time bison meat was needed, a new bison? No, all he had to do was to draw one again. Make once again the magic pass and the beast was already entangled by his magic line and foredoomed. Then the hunters could take part in the sacrament of identity and after the magic-artist had made again alive the figure, they might dart at it and so ensure its downfall to-morrow.

The hunting forecast, the foretelling of a fortunate adventure, tends now to become ritualised. Inevitably such day-dreaming gravitated toward the true time of the dream, the evening. Then you sat round the hearth at the cave's mouth and chorused your hopes, and, as the light faded and only the flickering embers lit up the depth of the cave, you could see the great magic animals on the walls actually lunge and stagger as to your chaunt the mystery art-man ran over the great beast's outlines and brought them to life and gave them to death. When afterwards you curled up for sleep you saw the very beast fall to earth and you knew that the magic of last night had ensured the *morte* of to-morrow. But gradually also you noticed that the great beasts drawn about the living part of the cave were not as alive as the fathers had said they were. At night they did move, but if you looked at them in the daylight, especially when the level light of the sun struck in on them, they were not real beasts, and sometimes in the morning you needed to have them alive, to know that you could magic into them the dreadful strength of the beast you must meet shortly in the open. But they remained stock still, and you knew that magic was not working, and when the hunt was disastrous and the hunters did not come back you realised that the picture had failed to draw into itself the beast's strength and so inevitably the tribe had been defeated. So the pictures farther back, in the deeper parts of the cave where the daylight never came, gained sanctity. Visit them at any time and raise your glimmering light and there they stood lowering at you from the walls. They were never dead or lacking in magic. And when you went to see them the mystery art-man not only could make them alive and dead as he wished, he himself could become like them. He disappeared into the dark, and the moment after there beside the living picture stood a terrible creature, half wild beast, half oneself. The picture moved on the wall but he stood out, came, making horrible sounds, toward the dedicating hunters. They fled in horror, but as they fled they felt a curious kinship had been made

between them and their prey. Totemism had arisen.[1]
The artist had taken a step toward the vestmented
priest. Yet it was no leap. The apes hang themselves with garlands. The ape men must have done
the same with pelts and tails and crests. It was but
a step for the artist to order such irrelevant additions
into a masquerade and for the rest to realise that
the dressed-up one was partaking of a double nature,
had become a bridge between them and their prey,
and was both their victim and their sustainer. So,
while still in the cave mouth, humanity has arrived
at the threshold of art, ritual and religion.

[1] See also p. 81.

CHAPTER II

THE EMERGENCE OF THE FULL MEN

I

AT the mouth of the cave, man shook off the last shackle of his animal nature. That is not to say that he ceased to be an animal. It is to maintain that when he left the cave after the gigantic trial and tribulation of the Ice Age, he left it as a unique animal. Not only would no other beast ever again dispute his mastery of the world, but his mastery should be so absolute and assured because it was henceforward to be, as had no other animal's, not by numbers, though these would follow, nor by strength, though this would become intense, nor even by cunning, but by the power, ever growing and ever more unnatural, of living in the future and seeing his present circumstances with a new detachment. Man was therefore henceforth free as had been no other animal. All the other species have been kept within the rigid rule of unconscious reaction. Presented with set circumstances their reply was set for them. They were experiments on the part of the Life Force, and so subordinated, so tentative that they have never known that they are experimental and that they serve race purposes of which they are the tools.

Man is still an experiment, but he divines that this is so. He is allowed to take an even more deliberate part in that experiment; and his destiny, and with it the destiny of life is put ever more completely in his hands. In him not only the life of his race but the consciousness of life itself becomes aware of itself. That this is so, even his anatomy shows. He is the only animal that has refused the lure of specialised efficiency. His hand, truest symbol of his power, is also best symbol of his freedom. In form it is still the unspecialised fronded feeler out of which the horses have hammered and hardened the swift hoof, the felines the rending paw, and even the birds the wing. Each specialisation gave to each species an immediate gift; but the stock of man

57

waited. It postponed victory in an immediate
province to have in the end suzerainty over the whole
empire of life.

The real history of man can therefore only be told
as the history of an emergence, and of an emergence
into an even fuller and more general awareness of
himself, of life and of the world. All his power and
vision are but consequences of his evolution, which
having preserved him physically uncommitted, now
evolves the fulfilment of that physical generality –
a mind that, age by age, increases its unique
capacity of seeing, not one selected series of useful
objects, but a greater and greater circle of general
observation, more and more things of which he
can only prophetically tell their use by saying that
they interest. Man had stood up to the ice. Neanderthal man had been crushed under that millennial
hardship. Yet, as the climate begins to raise its
curse, man begins to show that that energy which
had defied nature at its grimmest was almost too
much for him to control when no longer set and
balanced against inhuman forces. Neanderthal man,
whom he might have hated because he was another
species, is gone. But the creature of skill is not to
be at peace while Nature becomes again genial.
There is now only one species of man. Were he an
animal, he would not prey on his own species. He
shows that he is both higher and lower than a beast
by engaging increasingly in internecine struggle.

Neanderthal man gave way to the first neoanthropic men, the great artists of the Aurignacian Ages. And then from the East comes in a new people whose great station at Solutré has given them their name. Had the Aurignacs specialised too much in art and come to think too much that power lay purely in pictorial magic and not in the strength and skill the magic infused in them? Certainly the Solutreans seem to have adjusted the balance violently in the opposite direction. They have no such art as their predecessors whom they seem wholly to have dispossessed, but they had a specialised technique of weapon-making far in advance of anything known to man before. With such a perfected weapon-craft victory must have been theirs. But not peace. They specialised in weapons. They hunted down the small wild horse of the plains and feasted recklessly on his flesh. They were perfectly suited for that life so long as it should last, but it was a special life and they were too suited to profit by it to be able to provide against its failure. The fanciful, wasteful experiments that were to lead to pottery, to grain-raising, and to civilised life they had no need for the time to indulge, so successful were they. And the measure of their success in their immediate conditions was a measure of their failure when these changed.

And things now were changing as they had not changed for thousands of years. The ice was about to leave Europe. The climate we know was meliorating. Mankind, which had stood its ground, was now to be free to take over the large territories the ice was to yield, and all the southern territories he had known – the downlands of Arabia and the Sahara – were to change toward desert, driving him to the river valleys. The specialised Solutreans seem to disappear. Another age of Art Magic – the Magdalenian – succeeds them. The history of man as a generalised experimenter is resumed. It is succeeded by an age – the Azilean – when it would seem that man has become so varied in his accomplishments as to be no supreme master in any. Magic, it appears now, no longer needs for its efficacy naturalistic representations. It is worked by signs, drawn on pebbles. We are on the threshold of writing. A symbol is becoming valid for a picture. So we may suspect that the whole front of man's achievements is being linked up and brought forward into a single even line and extended. So this, the shortest of the old Stone Age epochs, closes that æon. The immense chapter of the Paleolithic, with all its hardship, endurance, and stolidity is over. The spring of the world is here again, and on its threshold stand the New Men. There is a swarming of physical movement and ideas. Humanity seethes. New ideas are everywhere and the original and the fantastic wins against the sound and the specialised. So the New Age we used to call the Neolithic enters upon the scene. Cultures that used to take millennia to pass by now are gone in as many centuries. The *tempo* of life is accelerated until we are almost at the pace when changes take place in a few generations, and so men can begin to be conscious of them. From that it is but a step for men to begin deliberately, and with a sense of what they are doing, themselves individually to make innovations and inventions.

But so full of contradictions is man that the very age of release is also the age of settlement. There is nothing more surprising at first sight than the distances that hunting man, after he had mastered his technique of weapon-making, managed to cover. Even the stones of the Neanderthal race are found scattered over three continents, and types of later styles, precisely similar to each other in every detail of technique, are found many thousands of miles apart. We forgot that though the early hunters could only move on foot they had at least a score of years for trekking, for all their active lives most of them had to be on the move.

As soon as the ice relaxed its grip they had to be out and after the droves of animals on which they hung and lived, as the Lapps to-day follow their reindeer. No doubt in their treks, grew up the companionship of man and dog, and finally the relationship of man and cattle. And then somewhere about 15,000 B.C. the ice sheets made their final retreat and man made his great advance forward: he settled down. Such a step, though it was of course led up to by the discovery of pottery and of grain, was nevertheless revolutionary. It was a sudden expansion of his mind that made it possible for him to concentrate. As Rousseau said, 'Only when you prevent a man acting will he then think.' As long as man could move, as long as the initiative was with his prey, the beasts followed the pastures and he the beasts. They set the pace and plan, and theirs was the prospect. Man as their camp-follower covered many countries, but with his circumscribed interest he saw little save the herd in whose tracks he trailed. At best he could but plan tactics – the movements of a skirmisher on the fringes of an army. But now he was to settle, to begin an intensive life, a life that, as it could not range widely in space, had to extend on into time. It was the sedentary way that made man reflective and led him to realise himself.

II

So history focuses and becomes clear, hot, intense under that focus. During the late Ice Age, man lived not too ill in caves and shelters around the upland springs on the downs, now desiccated and sand-swept by the Sahara. Along this great belt of land ranged the warm and rainy winds that now sweep North-west Europe. As the ice went north, so too the winds followed, the rains failed and the Sahara began. As the pools shrank and the vegetation withered man crept toward the upland edge. There one day some branch of men that had been edging unconsciously east for uncounted generations saw for the first time the first land of promise. For the lean uplands ended in a bluff and there below was spread the intense green of the Nile Valley. The contrast was striking. They had behind them barrenness. Immediately ahead lay luxuriance. The growing heat of the sun that had parched the upland made this river-soaked cleft dense with plenty. As they crept down, they pushed their way through abundant fruits, dense flocks of birds rose under their feet and though the serpent hissed and the leopard snarled, countless other animals scattered at their approach and showed how rich a repast Nature had here spread before them.

So man, the wanderer, came to his home, and as he settled the whirl of days settled also and he began to know time. As he abode on the edge of the valley, night by night he saw the same moon rise over the desert edge, and yet each day in detail it had changed. For many years the sky repeated to man that simple lesson, that sky which was unconfined by clouds and in which the moon ran clear cut its unobscured course. The sun was always the same and too much the source of all vision and the summoner to tasks he pointed out, himself to be watched, but when day was over and the people sat in the cool of the evening, the moon was the perfect object of detached interest. Each evening it was there, but each evening it was changed. It grew daily less until that day when it was not, and then after a day or two it grew up again from a curve fine as a shell sliver to its full orb that could flood the valley with light; and so back again into the darkness. Here was a cycle quite definite and not too long to be recalled. Here was a face that arrested attention and which in distinctly recognisable stages told its age. Man's time range extended to the month and he was master of a mass of thirty days.

And that land of remembrance also taught him not to forget in another way. Before this he had learnt to put away his dead and with them what they had used. Animals when they give birth devour the placenta. Many of them regularly clean their lairs. To leave a dead member close by the hearth was obviously at animal level, intolerable, and as his weapons were part of him it needed an exercise of reason, little less violent than that now needed to give the body of a dear friend to the dissectors, to take and use his tools. There is no need as yet to postulate a belief in a future life from such burials. Many a woman is buried to-day with her wedding ring though she realises that after death there is no 'marrying or giving in marriage,' but for the ancient feeling that inspired first man, not to sunder from the dead what had been so identified with them.

But now he was to bury and to remember as he had not before. The dry sand of the desert preserved his dead. He knew this was so, not because he looted the graves but because the jackal did. He must again and again have surprised these scavengers at their work, and there instead of unrecognisable bones lay the body hardly changed. He must often have reflected on this often repeated resurrection. Sometimes, no doubt, he saw the jackal making off in the moonlight with the limbs, a ghastly sight we think. But, separated in acute individuality, we underrate the mythic and sympathetic power of man's mind when still close to the animal world. No, he felt that the mysterious beast which sat about his bounds, watching him in the dark with gleaming eyes, calling to him but moving away when he approached, this animal, whom he surprised in contact with the dead, was no scavenger, no ghoul. It was a mysterious power that somehow had dealings with the dead and, he concluded, was leading them into that other world to which they were addressed. For this was his conclusion as we can see from the most impressive and persistent series of death pictures any race has ever left. In every picture of the soul before Osiris we see that it is ushered into the presence of the Supreme Judge by the Messenger of the Gods, Anubis of the jackal head.

So man could not forget his dead. He felt that though they had taken their gear with them they had not gone away. They resided about his dwellings, and, as he changed but they endured, as he realised gradually his individuality, and with that realisation his ephemerality, they became the repository of his tradition and the guarantee of the people's persistence. The living must pass, but so long as the dead remained the people should endure. So he built them houses such as his own houses, that they too might live in his sight. At first he sheathed the sand pit in which they lay with boarding to give them room. Then he built steps down to that room that he might visit them. Finally, but that is later than the stage we have now come to in this survey, above the underground room he will rear a house copying in enduring stone the fragile reed posts and screens of his own transitory dwellings.

As his time sense increased and as the climate of his valley home provoked that increase, so the dead became increasingly his companions. They were not dead, he felt. They were living alongside of him, and as they did not grow old as those who remained grew old, he gradually came to think of them as not less but more alive than the living. The dead become the enduring reality of the group-life, of which the living were only the flickering appearance.

But as man's speculation grew, a third definition began to appear united with his two other speculations to make the threefold basis of his civilisation. The clear moon that went through its story in thirty days had extended his time sense to a month's span. The undecaying dead had extended his thought beyond death. So he realised the community going on eternally. Together Death and Time made the first civilised man realise the strength of his society and not, as an individual would assume, the worthlessness of his own momentary emergence on the scene. As the looting jackal gave him not a thrill of disgust, but a fancy of resurrection, so the realisation of Death and Time, instead of provoking doubts as to his private destiny, made him certain that the people endured.

So his consciousness opened, not on to a grey and desolate landscape, but on to a golden prospect, and this same optimism is shown in the third stage of his thought's definition, his speculation as to how the living community endured and how it was kept in touch with the holy and eternal dead. The sub-human groups can have had no traditions, but we know from the study of apes how strong is the sub-rational, sub-individualistic tie that binds them together. So man must first have been bound up in the life of this group. But with an extending, intensifying consciousness, which, it has been suggested, the Moon and the dead provoked, he would become aware that the Group was not a thing itself, but only an aggregate of individuals like himself. He felt in himself urge to experiment, to devagate, even to wonder in an unsettling way. The still unconscious wish to keep himself safe with the group, to be saved from the disruptive insulating tendencies in himself, would therefore throw up the individual Sovereignty. For this is the inevitable individualised expression and concentration of the elder sense of the Group, which was originally directly diffused among all its constituents.

We cannot say for certainty whether the Mother

or the Father idea first crystallised round itself the Group loyalty, no longer to be held in general solution. But there is much to be said in favour of the notion that Motherhood ideas more closely define the feeling-force of an early group than do the ideas associated with Fatherhood. And we know that in Egypt no Pharaoh could wear the holy crown till he had consummated marriage with a wife through whom he seems to have inherited the throne. Woman is the Gate of Life. The tribe realised itself as the emergent phase of an eternal cycle of birth and death. If the dead first gave man cultural continuity, the birth-giver would be their natural complement, the other centre round which the orbit of life swung. And growing individuality among the Group would project itself by a growing individualisation of what was worshipped. Motherhood would be worshipped in one Great Mother in which the rest were assumed. She would be plenty and power. So Hathor the Sacred Cow becomes Mother of the Land and when the rulership becomes male, she is suckler of Pharaoh; and even the force of destruction, Sektmet, is conceived, not as male but as a lioness. Whether male or female, that individual, who was henceforward worshipped as the incarnation of the Group, ruled through relationship with the potentiality rather than with the actuality of life. It was that force which first gave the ruler authority, because it is not physical coercion that keeps an animal pack together, any more than it is a clear-sighted balance of the profits and costs of such a union that makes the constituents cohere.

The first ruler is therefore a being whose attributes are such that they all become, with the growing definition of an intensifying consciousness, magical. This being is no tyrant or one with whom men made contracts, or even a hero who promises them deliverance and dominance. She or he is a sacramental creature, a mystic concentration of the tribe's actuality and a mystic link with the potentiality of the other life.

III

So civilisation begins, not in conquest or subjection – though these disturbing factors are soon intermixed – but through the growing self-consciousness of the units of the group. Moral and political order is but the accentuation and deliberate emphasis of what, in the animal and the half-human societies, is a spontaneous organisation. This, then, is the first picture we can have of civilised man. We find him seated by the banks of the Nile gathered in a ring of huts made of reed mats held by bound bundles of reed. In the centre is a larger dwelling, firmer and ampler. Here dwells the person who is identified with the tribe's very soul. The days pass more pleasantly, if more straitly, than they did. Mark of civilisation, there is greater plenty, but more to do. There are tasks set but there is infinite energy

69

only asking to be directed. So the soft translucent alabaster is ground into bowls, and then the hard diorite, and pottery is shaped and baked, at first by the sun. And man who carries in him the ape's passion for grooming, spends long delightful hours grooming himself, oiling his skin and hair. He daubs himself with the coloured powders that the ground stones left, he finds the vivid malachite and sees how well its green shows upon his native brown. He notices that the green stain remains on his skin. He finds a queer quaint pleasure in pricking his skin and rubbing in shrub juices. He finds intenser pleasure in piercing his ear-lobes and lips. He is deeply entertained at being able to add to or prune this strange body of his. Scornfully has the historian looked down upon such trivialities. Is not history either the acts of heroes or 'the crimes, the follies, and the misfortunes of mankind'? Is not the Scroll of Time only to be filled by worthy incident, tragic or majestic? What part in a comprehensive chronology can have cosmetics? Yet cosmetics can be an acid test of our true detachment – indeed of our power to view man, if not *sub specie aeternitatis*, at least as a single unbroken process.

Perhaps (as will be suggested later in this book, when the Historian Age is reached) historians themselves recapitulate history. Certain it is that to this psychological age cosmetics can be illuminating. For the flower and the animal, though they may be arrayed more splendidly than Solomon, are not conscious of their array and as we study it we find that splendour may be as utilitarian, as purposive, as fustian or khaki. As we have learnt to look into it with understanding we see there is no extravagance about it. Much of it actually serves as a disguise and to cause the animal to be unnoticed and sink into its background. The late war showed that a dazzling motley may be a far better disguise than the drabbest uniform. Many of the most splendid liveries of nature are really complete obliterations of form. For the rest, colour, when not hiding you from your enemies, is a signal to your friends. It is a spontaneous signpost over your door telling those in similar line of business that you have goods to exchange. But with the ape and his dawn consciousness we get personal emphasis. A swaith of creeper is worn to amplify his sense of individual being.

And so when we come to man we can see how indicative his personal decoration may be of his growth and degree of self-consciousness. In his animal state he does not define between himself and his desires, and as his desires are largely in the world outside himself, he does not realise the gap that yawns between himself and the outer world where lie so many of his goals. Survivals of that primal mentality hang on in religion, wherever sympathetic magic still is worked, because man began by being unable to distinguish between his own actions and the movements of the outer world. So he assumes that when he spits and the saliva falls back in his face, the sky, too, will begin to spit rain, and that when he leaps high the grasses will grow tall. And so every child must recapitulate that experience crying for the moon, fancying that the pillar-box, behind which it stands concealed, is really larger than the dome of the cathedral in the background.

Indeed the one underlying and unifying theme of all history is man's growth in power and objectivity, in his power to see things with increasing detachment from the particular viewpoint at which for the moment he personally rests.

The use of and interest in cosmetics is, then, important, because is shows man become in a new, intense and individual way, aware of his body, of its peculiar, unique position to himself; of his intensified sense of personal identity.

The time man spends on personal decoration is then not vanity and folly. On the contrary it is the way in which he learns to distinguish what he is from what he desires. And as he satisfies his sense of decoration, and his desire to exercise power through alteration, so he realises his position, and with tattoo print and cosmetic brush, etches and paints that, the frontier of all frontiers, which till then he had confused, that lies between direct consciousness and control, and all that lies beyond.

As we make up our body it helps us to make up our minds: to realise that there is this great gulf fixed between our physique and all the rest of the physical creation. So cosmetics show that the racial day-dream is ending, and through vanity man becomes a realist.

Such a dawning consciousness must soon extend until it reached to and lit up further frontiers. The dawning self-awareness that causes personal decoration, and which personal decoration in turn makes more acute, makes man not only aware of an intense distinctness of place – that his body is his own and no one else's – but also of a distinct awareness of time. He realises that his body changes. Teeth and hair, once intensely in touch, become detached. The limbs grow stiff and break, the eyes grow dim. He has come to the loneliness of individuality – that no one else can share his bodily pain. Thence he must go on to the greater loneliness when, having learnt to love his individuality, he dreads its loss and thinks with panic that no one else can share his unconsciousness and death.

In some such way knowledge and realisation of death, as something that he could not escape, would prise its way into his closed life. He might refuse to realise the fact until one day the chief person would ail and die. They did not have to wait till she moved no more to know that she was dead. Her life was the life of the community and so inevitably its only valid sign was the power of reproduction. When that failed, if the heart and lungs still moved they were unnatural and should be stilled; they could only maintain a mockery of life, a living death, a creature now existing no longer for all but for its pointless self alone. Such an unnaturalness must be cut off and the choked current of life find another clear and clean channel. But there was no hate nor bitterness in this correction. She who had centred in herself the abiding power of the race, she whose permanence made other deaths but ripples on the full pool, she had withdrawn. But life had not failed. A fresh body and manifestation would show forth the present life. The elder form would be taken where it would no more decay and where therefore it would be obvious symbol of that latent, inherent, eternal life from which the forms of the day rise and to which they return. Therefore the tribe carried the dead priestess-queen to the town of the dead, past the simple shafts in which lay ordinary people, to the Great House in the centre. This, as became the house of eternity, fulfilled in brick and stone the reed structure of the home of life. There under its rooms the people's Luck was laid and a successor reigned in the house of manifest life among those who were in that day of the upper world. But with those who reigned below, the living left offerings. They gave drink and meat and the best seeds of the choice wild barley which grew abundantly of itself in this Valley. So it was that they realised and accepted death, and though they might not draw its sting they rendered themselves largely immune to its poison.

And so also it was, when they visited again, behold

though the drink had vanished and the meat shrunken to a casting, some of the seeds had sprouted. So the harvest was evidently grown by the divine leader. Man had direct proof of his belief, argument for his conviction, that she lived in a way the others did not live, because she caused the barley to spring. So man learned to save and bury some grains every year; trusting that the great dead would accept them and from below send up again with the spring a hundredfold in return.

At first agriculture was restricted to graveyard tillage. Man was still mainly a food-gatherer, depending thoughtlessly on the abundance of the wild barley. But generation after generation as he despoiled the wild fields and they yielded less, so compensatingly extended the sacred enclosure of sepulchrally sown barley. More and more ate the sacred corn and worked for the holy acres. These spread, until the fertilising magic of the dead leader was recognised to extend to every fruitful field in the whole valley. All grain deliberately grown was sacred. It all sprang from the holy will and efficacy of the divine being placed underground.

There is no revolution or break in early man's life. No violence is done to his soul but, holding fast to the clue of his tradition, he finds that it unspins in his hand, as step by step, he advances. So in Egypt, so, too, in Mesopotamia and in the Indus Valley: the little settlements grow into towns and the towns to cities. These atomic systems of

75

society are marvellously stable but a process of concentration and specialisation goes on. So, as it were from a great height, we have surveyed man emerging to full manhood. We have seen him come out of the tree, still largely an ape, still without gear or traditions. We have seen him go into the Ice Age, to emerge from the Caves into which it drove him, clothed and armed. We have seen the retreating Ice draw after it the rains; his upland stations become desert and the river valleys receive him: the valley, the third mould of environment in which he will take his further shape as a full man. In the Tree he became the Super-Ape. In the cave he became the Group Man. In the river valley he became the tillage-town's man. He is now and henceforward, in the river valleys of the Indus and of Mesopotamia and of the Nile, a person of traditions. So far a common drive has made him spring, though from three jets, in a common current. Thenceforward as the rush of life rises ever higher, as a fountain breaks into a spreading crest of droplets, so these three currents will vary and in themselves become broken up. But still through all the whirl and spray of civilisation the informing drive of a single emergent mind can be detected and from that current we can understand and interpret what is otherwise a copious confusion.

Now we must begin our descent. We must begin to come closer to earth, to the actual sites, villages and houses of men. For now the speed of history is so accelerated that we do not need to stand back so far and to take in so vast a span of time to recognise that there is a single movement going on. Almost on the scale of a single society, soon on the scale of a single generation will change be detectable.

Yet we must begin this new phase standing almost as high above the world, as far above that level at which individuals become perceptible, as we were in the last chapter.

So we look down.

CHAPTER III

THE DAWN OF CULTURE

I

THE clouds reopen and from the heaven of history we again survey, as one creature, Mankind. We see the great Shoulder of the Globe before us. Round its Neck we still see the icy mantle of the glaciers and snowfields, a hood that still shrouds what is, to-day,

78

the temperate North, and below that hood spreads
a deep fringe of rain belt, hanging above a sodden
and harrowed land, filling little lakes whose isth-
muses are dense with tangled pine. An icy swamp
and lagoon land, for the water-rats and the beavers,
but not for Man. South again lies the temperate
climate, the natural home of Man. We see the
Sahara, a great downland with uplands already
becoming sparse like the uplands of Spain. On this
upland, from the Atlas to the shores that stretched
from Susa round to Kharachi, we still may see men
carrying on the Stone Age life of the food-gatherer.
They camp round the shrinking water holes and are
become skilful in catching the birds and animals that
must come there to drink. They are also become
cunning in digging for roots and finding berries; but
life is against them and their steady growth in skill
is always met by a shrinkage of supplies. One
thread holds them above destruction. The open
land is loved by animals that live by the power to
outpace all pursuit.

To some of these the man of the upland managed
to attach himself. As millennia before, men had hung
about the trailing herds of oxen, so now these
laggards of mankind would fall back and pick up
with horse herds and camel flocks. Man has always
felt a strange kinship between himself and the
animal. The life in him cries out that here is he
himself only in other form. He divines by living
sympathy the truth later revealed by comparative

anatomy that all living forms are but variants of one body which expresses the comprehensive will to live. So as the jackal became to the first sexton in the river valley, the completer of his rite instead of the ravisher of his work, so horse and camel became companionite with the man of the water hole. He saw the young suck the mares, and he, too, with imitation and enterprise sucked first those mares who had lost their foals, and then from every full udder. This is the pipeline which keeps on the men of the steppe, the first specialisations of human society, the first social atavisms, from whom were to spring the barbarian invaders, who, until to-day, men were to assume as the invariable contrast of civilisation and its probable supplanter. Here is one of the paradoxes of history that the Man of War is a Man of Milk.

That civilisation, as we have seen, is already springing in the river valleys. As we look down, it is on these Clefts we must focus, for here the destiny of man is at issue. We see the three great valleys, Nile, Euphrates and Indus, and on each we see similar small settlements where life has intensified by settling. What is the process? Let us mark its outward stages and then from them attempt to diagnose the cause. We have seen the Group growing defined and stratified. First by self-decoration it learns, unawarely, but clearly, to take that great step which separates it off from all the world in which it lives. Its body, it learns by tattoo, brand and stain, is separate from everything else. And definition once started, must continue. Sacred areas of the body are demarcated, so they are focused in consciousness and stay there memorised when the inner monitor of sensation is silent. So man's consciousness of his physiology ceases to be intermittent[1] and becomes continuous and those individuals who are most sacred, they are marked out. So classes arise. But classes are not mere sunderings of the primal unconscious unity: they extend it also. If the Great Mother wears clothes of feathers so that she brood over the whole tribe in sacred fecund contemplation, she assumes in her nature something of the mystery of bird life, and though this mystery makes her as a woman alien, it draws all birds from their shy and airy distance somehow into the tribe's ambit.

So classification not only defines, it also enlarges, and man, through the Totem – a fancy which we have seen he already played with in the cave[2] – makes bridges whereby, as he becomes more civilised, he shall not become, through loss of unconscious animalism, completely out of touch with the other animate world, or even with the inanimate.

So we have the first stage of social thought – classes defined more by paint than by patent, and the class, though defining the stratification of

[1] The loss of the sexual periodicity which all other animals have, must have been the beginning of his sense of continuity.

[2] See p. 55.

society, yet, at the same time, extending humanity to the animals.

And the same social settlement that provoked man to trace the first boundaries of his constitution on his body, permitted him also to improve by reflection and experiment his tools, his gear and his dwellings. We must repeat that the first and necessary step toward the new quick way of civilisation was that he should settle down. As we recognise how it is the settled societies that have gone forward, the roving societies that have stayed still, we see illustrated again the truth: 'Man only thinks when you prevent him from acting.' For by being settled in one place he came again and again on the same thing altered in no way save by time. He saw things at last almost under laboratory conditions. For the wanderer from water hole to water hole the world was a huge confusion. He could reflect as little as the bird which, when startled, flies so fast away that when it comes to rest there is little to remind it as to what provoked its flight. So as the man of the settlement had seen night after night the crescent moon, he came to notice day after day the mud in which he had stuck his toe harden and become a cast, the mud river foreshore of itself crack and be baked into natural bricks ready for the picking. Pottery and brickwork came to him without his deliberate intention. And hard on the sun-baked pot and brick came the fire-baked pot and brick. And he who knapped the brittle flint and shaped the soft clay soon, as we have seen, found the soft and lustrous alabaster that may be scooped into vessels like clay vessels but needing no baking. While alabaster itself was a bridge that led him to grind and shape and scoop diorite and granite. And each advance gave him not only more to handle, but more to think about. If he could act with new materials in so many new ways, why should he be so stereotyped in his social actions? That was the question that discovery was provoking in his mind, and though he could not frame it in speech or thought, yet, as he gained power to persist at long and toilsome work, of fashioning shapes out of hard material, so he gained power of brooding and returning to his other problems. Why did he respect Motherhood? What was there great about the female? To the more restless these problems recurred. It was the search for Sanctions. Was man serving and fearing sanctity for naught? So the *Mana* of the creative life of the tribe, first probably focused on the woman, had next to be vicariously manifested by her surrogate the priest-king. This is the stage of which we first find historic record. It is at this stage of man's emergence that we find the pre-dynastic totem kinglets of Egypt, the proto-patesis of Mesopotamia and the primal rulers of Harappa and Mohenjo Daro in the Indus Valley. That an earlier stage lies behind, that in that stage the accent was increasingly, as we go backward, on the priest rather than on the king, and that such a stage must be prehistoric, because it enjoys the happiness that has no annals, all this is not only probable, but we see the reason for it when we realise that what we have been watching is in the first, annal-less, part, an unconscious evolution, and in the second part the on-coming of conscious departures and deliberate innovations. In short, all the development of protocivilisation is indicative and symptomatic of a slow intensification of consciousness which at a certain point emerged over the threshold. The clue to this æon is a revolution in the mind. Man is changed from a being predominantly social to be a being predominantly self-conscious and individual. Yet the process of emergence will not run smooth. Society must hold itself together against a headlong swarming forth of individuals, in which society would have disappeared.

II

Hence the rise of the kingship is inevitable; for the king is indicative of individualism, individualism which first frees itself and then dominates the rest; while the Great Mother is indicative of the homogeneous tribe which is predominantly conscious of its continuity through procreation. But the change is slow. It is a revolution, but one counted not by days, but by scores of generations. The first stage is to transfer the holiness of the woman to the man, and so transform a disruptive individual into a social band. So he lives a transitional being. Such we may imagine must have been the first kings. They would have to submit to nearly all the limitations which came quite naturally to the Great Mother. In her it was natural that She should live secluded days, her life parcelled and quartered by sacredness, she and the Moon keeping pace in a cosmic pavane, passing and repassing from the fully manifest to the high potential of complete secrecy. And inevitable with her nature was it that when she definitely ceased to bring forth that she should be ritually put out. The individual body was as naught. It was the incarnating spirit of the tribal life that made her sacred and when it removed, then the husk must be cleared away, even as the snuff-choked wick of the lamp is trimmed that the sinking flame may again burn up clearly.

But such a ritual of renunciation when imposed on a king could but be transitional. Hence the kings fly to an original action. They take to war, war that will free them from the jealous magic of the tribe, war that will make the tribe depend on their individual power and not on them as simply the charged but passive terminal of the tribe's vitality. And the people also are ready for war. For they, too, have become conscious enough to wish to try new ways, to wish definitely for adventure, for risk, for uncovenanted and sudden advantage. They desire to challenge sacred unmoving authority. They realise suddenly with resentment that they move and it remains. For the accent now is changing. Earlier, we have seen, the tribe's persistence was a comfort to the constituent. It staunched and assuaged the intensifying sense of his fleetingness. Now, however, that sense has become so acute that the fact that the tribe survives him is no longer assuagement but an added bitterness. They throw their lot in with the adventurer, the pioneer, the pirate.

Yet can they not be complete realists. War itself has its evolution, because it is part of man's evolution. Primal war is that stage when man's self-consciousness is such that he has to confirm magic with physical violence. Gradually that balance will shift, but never to the present day, and perhaps never as long as man fights, will the appeal be only to arms. Men reasonable enough not to mix their appeal to force with an appeal to luck, will be reasonable enough not to fight. So we see the first kings go out to fight. We have from his cosmetic palate, off which he made himself up, the picture of that far from primal king, Narmer of Egypt.[1] He leads his troops to bloody victory, but he does so not merely by the strength of his right arm and the weight of his mace, but through the terrific influence of the Falcon Totem that flies over him. To it, high god of battles, is the glory, to man only the gain. For it, in the unseen, overthrew the *Mana* of the Cat

[1] Probably of Lower Egypt and perhaps immediate predecessor to Mena who united Upper and Lower Egypt into the one land.

and of the other Totems and brought them down.
But though the Cat's people were killed and per-
chance the Cat herself taken, she was not conquered, and to kill her would be for man blas-
phemously and sacrilegiously to enter on the dis-
putes of the high gods. And what avails it to destroy
her body only to release her terrible soul which with
green eyes would stalk the soul of the King, who at
night must fly before it as a mouse? So the Cat Bes
joins with Falcon Horus, and so the parish kingdoms
come together and the hierarchy of heaven swells.
But the adding of Nome to Nome is only a symptom
and consequence of the spread of Man's ideas. As
soon as he becomes capable of conceiving a society
greater than that of his parish and its market-town,
so soon does a real kingdom appear. So the rise of
the true kingdom, of the many cities ruled by one
commander, is shown in the Standards. Horus,
which was once only the Hawk Totem of a parochial
Nome, now becomes associated with the Sun, close
against which his watchers have seen him fly, and
once he and the Sun are united, his people have
right, as Vicegerents of the Sun, to a kingdom as
wide of the Sun's.

We see then a tripartite growth going on among
men. The political, social, national growth is one
aspect, but it is only the manifest symptom of the
other sides. These are man's growing sense of the
world around him and his growing knowledge of
himself. Without the growth of these two senses

there would have been no history, political or social. That outward history is but a consequence of conclusions reached in these two deeper fields. And in the first banners of Egypt the three sides of his nature and interest are displayed. We see the totem banners marking, first his mysterious sense of life's unity; later, as that is lost, to become heraldic symbols of political alliance. We see to the totem banners added the standard of the Moon and later of the Sun indicative that Man's conception of the outer world goes beyond animal, even beyond the vegetable, to the inorganic. And as his vision extends so his grasp will be extended – he will wish to know and control all that Sun and Moon know and survey, and from them he will slowly gain a sense of order so that his conception of law will show a sense of that invariability and indifference which is the technique of justice. But among his banners we see a third, indefinite but persistent. This marks the Third Estate of Man's strange kingdom of the Mind. There is the inanimate world, there is also the world of living forms outside him; but there is a third division of his interest. There is his strange body, so intimately alive and his, and yet so alien, so uncontrollable. So the Third Estate of the Standard is the Standard of his members. There is hoisted the mysterious 'Bundle of Life,' the placental coil, and there, too, beside it its phallic complement. As this predynastic procession moves forward we see how in its symbols it reveals how the mind of man, addressed to conquest, advances. So it keeps in touch with a united past of experience, for here, in order, we have contact with body, with animal life and with the larger Nature beyond animal life. And so also it keeps in touch, its lines of communication unbroken, with all its past, even large conceptions of man, of life, of Nature, growing and sprouting from the simplest and smallest fancies.

It is this need to keep in touch with the past and not to root up and rupture the continuity of living that we now see accounts for the delays and recapitulations of history. Looking at it, as narrow individualised rationalists, men have often wondered and despaired at the slow, tentative and stumbling manner in which man has advanced. So men marvelled that man could not be nourished on synthetic food, not knowing of vitamins. Probably, with all its elaboration, history has advanced with the least possible delay, society has sustained itself with the least extravagant expenditure of energy or elaboration of forms, and man has emerged as quickly as was possible, without complete disaster.

So it is, and so only, that we may interpret the fact, that every stage of advance is followed by one of consolidation: that every romantic age in love with Nature must be intercalated with a classic age devoted to style: that every advance in knowledge of the outer world is related exactly to a change in man's consciousness and must so lead to a change in human society.

III

We have reached the threshold of history. The time is some seven thousand years ago. The little sparks of culture that gleamed from the tiny cities of the Indus Valley, of Mesopotamia and of the Nile have each in their valley spread until, along the banks of these great rivers, a glow extended. The same process is at work in each. Indeed we need scarcely ask where started the thing. Certain notions are inevitable, and whether the forms in which they found their expression were handed round the world or whether like questions led to like answers, the fact remains that if to all men the same problem had not presented itself they could not have adopted the same solution. The common language of symbol was possible – whether diffused from one source or springing from several sources – because the experience which it interpreted was common to all mankind. So the description of Egypt (which has kept in perfect dessication its unbroken record from then till now) gives us the outline of all other early cultures, for not till the emergence of full self-consciousness and its consequences, deliberate inventions, departures and discoveries, will men, in however different circumstances, have fundamentally a different conduct. Knowledge of the outer world is related exactly to a change in man's consciousness and must so lead to a change in human society. So what we find in

Egypt we can take to be the story of civilisation told
in Egyptian. When we translate that and under its
local accent take the meaning, we have as well the
meaning and substance of all the other local variants
of civilisation. And here we see the age of advance
followed by the age of consolidation. Egypt had
already gone up two flights of culture from the level
of the simple group. First came the Nomes and then
the Two Kingdoms. We have had a glimpse of the
Nomes, let us glance a moment at the Kingdoms.
The Nomes left only traces – such as the heraldry
and pantheon – in the life of historic Egypt, but the
Two Kingdoms remain through the history of
Egypt, a diversion as distinct as the sutures of a
skull: fusion took place but the line of demarcation
was never obliterated. These marks of earlier
divisions are as important and illuminating in
history as are the marks of fusion in the human body.
We may say that wherever they are strong enough to
resist complete obliteration through the later growth
of unification, they are so because they mark a
threshold where human society rested at a formative
period before it could summon sufficient strength to
achieve a larger unity. Human society advances
because man pulls himself together. The society
advances sporadically because these contractions,
condensations, focusings of the human spirit are
sudden, and before and after them there is rest. The
attainment of kingdom status is of course in itself a
great effort and remarkable achievement. We who

are impatient at the federalisation of our Europe can comfort ourselves by looking back. For the city state could be attained almost imperceptibly, but beyond that a deliberate policy was needed. It was not enough for city to raid city or even for a city king, active, individual, resourceful, to unite several cities. How should an individual, of all people, make widely scattered thousands think of the land as theirs, shared between them all? How should one city not only hold down the rest but be borne up by them? Here, then, we see the double process which has made civilisation possible in the past, and which makes a future for it a not unreasonable hope. For while man has grown individual, so, too, being freed from his concentration on his original group, he can conceive of larger, if more lightly held, loyalties. His reason, too, is by his self-consciousness awoken, and whereas, in his less rational stage the range of his senses was the limit of his emotions, and the limit of his emotions bounded his power to achieve, now he begins to be able to alloy his unreflecting devotion with a sense of business and with a realisation of the convenience of a unit larger than the spontaneous city. He begins to be able to stretch his emotions to suit his convenience, and, like a true politician, to be able to feel patriotism as far as the tributaries of his pocket extend. So Egypt sees a king of the South who in his traffic-cleft reigns, bearing the white mitre and controlling the commerce of Nubia with its gold and ivory and of the

Red Sea coastal belt with its crops and textiles, food, raiment, weapons and wares. And on the rich delta mouth also there springs to the call of unity another king who under his red cap, forerunner of the doge's, unites coasters and traders, rich alluvial farmers and busy manufacturers. Such kingdoms could not remain. Their very success led to their collision and their fusion in a larger unit. But because they were the first kingdoms, because they were the units in which man first conceived of a social life which was not traditional and inevitable but alloyed with enterprise and modified by convenience, they remained for ever in the minds of men, even when long outgrown, as the very idea of kingdom. So the Pharaoh, though he rules an Egypt which realises itself as one, still wears the double crown – the two diadems blended into a single tiara, and though he conquers countries far beyond the frontiers of the two kingdoms his crown remains, as though achievement could go no further, as it was the day when the two primal kingdoms were able to realise themselves as the one Land.

That this double diadem may indeed mark a frontier in the social evolution of man is suggested by the fact that in Mesopotamia there was also, after the day of the City States ruled by their priest-king Patesis, a stage of double kingdom, for there was the upper Kingdom of Akkad and the lower of Sumer. While on the Indus, the Sind civilisation seems also to have had two regional centres, the one centred at Harappa and the other at Mohenjo Daro. The achievement of kingdom-age is, as has been said, not to be attained without great effort on the part of all. The king must show enterprise and yet be no adventurer, for if his work is to last he must care as much for conserving what he has won as he has cared to win it. Like a true strategist having broken through the line of opposition, he must not plunge headlong forward but must turn and stabilise on the new enlarged front. The peoples must be prepared to weaken greatly their hold on the sacred past, that living sense of the community's eternal unchanging life. They must break innumerable sustaining taboos. They must concentrate their thoughts on the material advantages that will accrue to them through the larger secularised life they will live. Yet they must not be purely rational or materialistic. They must still venerate the community with a devotion which from the purely individualistic point of view is irrational. If they fail to feel this, if their rationalism becomes complete, then the community is doomed. So a balance has to be maintained between two moods, and this gives rise to mental conflict. In the face of such facts we should rather be surprised that humanity advances at all than that its advance is intermittent. The mental exhaustion brought about by the divided loyalty cannot be indefinitely postponed and in consequence each age of expansion and advance is followed by an age which has been called an age of decadence. Such a name could only be used by those who have failed to realise that all advance is made by mental effort and that such effort cannot be unremitting. It is not decadent to recuperate. Winter is not the decadence of summer. Rest and recuperative periods are essential phases of advance. The mental resources of society are recharged, and the advanced positions are consolidated. Man has to get used to his new condition. He has to make endless adjustments to sustain his social life at this new level. He has to become acclimatised to each higher stage of civilisation as his physique has become acclimatised to conditions which, to primitive life, would have proved fatal.

So the history of kingship seems, outwardly, a series of heroic break-aways always followed by a series of recaptures and reimprisonments by the priesthood. If we consider society as the outward physical symptom of an evolution of mental co-ordinations and associations, we see, however, that the king is the indicator of the community's alternating advance.

IV

It is therefore on this, the threshold of history, that we can trace those alternations which our epoch has called the Classic and the Romantic. The romantic period is when the leader breaks away and drawing like-minded followers initiates a campaign of advance. The classic period succeeds this inevitably, when the pent energies that cause enterprise become exhausted, and men therefore again feel that what they want is security. When this classic period comes on, the king is, as it were, recaptured. The priesthood reasserts its rights and the chief ruler is re-ceremented by tabus into a ritual figure. This alternating process is clearly illustrated throughout the history of Egypt. The Pharaoh after every phase of initiative sinks back to become the passive priest-tended Luck of the Land. Yet the process is not an aimless alternation. Rather the two points make the double centre round which there turns the spiral of man's advance. In the Third Dynasty – after the great expansive moments which had blended the Two Kingdoms and made Egypt one – we find the eminent Pharaoh Zozer. His name is The Holy, and such a title must indicate that here lies, after the steep and exhausting ascent of social advance and expansion, a level platform of recollection. Yet though this revived priest-king rules mainly through his vizier and may well himself have been the unmoving centre round which the enlarged social organism learnt to follow an orderly sequence, this age is not an age of sterility. It is better recognised as an age of crystallisation. For that word describes exactly what was taking place. Men were learning how to make permanent and how to consolidate, how to give perfect form to what had been in flux; tentative, provisional, temporary, amateur. Of this we have the clearest evidence. For in the tomb of Zozer himself we find, thousands of years before the mathematic Greeks recognised its geometric beauty and made it known as the Doric column, the fluted pillar and here at its rise we can recognise its real nature. It is the bundle of reeds – the weak door-post with which the hut dwellers had to be content, made everlasting by being worked in stone. And round the chamber of this dawn classic age are also other petrifactions of the simple frail life of that day – for the walls are patiently diapered in hard stone and tile to give a fossilisation of the reed-mat sides of the living dwellings of that day.

So the thought of man advances and leaves these prints whereby we may reconstruct its path and measure how it has grown as it has come upon its journey. So we may trace man's emergence. The first man of action was still a magician. But gradually action and magic become incompatible. Then each time the man of action breaks away from the toils he becomes more and more the soldier whose power is in his arms and less and less a mystery-monger whose authority resides in his *mana*. And each time the toils recapture him the less is he a magician and the more simply a passive luck. So we can see how the king can become a victim and during these classic periods have to suffer the ritual execution which, we have seen, naturally befalls the Holy Mother who can no longer bear. But the fact that his execution *is* itself a ritual, ends in his salvation. For ritual acts need not be actual. The growing sense that they are sacramental leads to the sacrifice becoming nominal. An act, the significance of which lies increasingly in another world, decreasingly has reality in this. The most ritualised king may then live out his days. And of this process, whereby the living man is kept in this living world, but his grace and power and influence are made still to keep the other world and this in touch, of this we have the actual evidence in the full Egyptian record. The Pharaoh learnt ritually to put on immortality. At the Sed festival which took place after he had reigned a certain number of years he went through a ritual death and resurrection, and there can be no doubt that this festival is the vestige of a real sacrifice when the death putting was actual. Of this we have other evidence, for as late as the Sixth Dynasty there still existed in Egypt an officer called the Opener of the Placenta. This officer originally killed the Pharaoh, for the opening of this sacred Bundle of Life, which we have seen prominent among the nation's ensigns, meant the release of the soul which till then tabernacled among men on this side of the Veil. By the Sixth Dynasty a vicarious victim is found, and in the New Kingdom – an epoch of realistic romance and expansion – the title, naturally, became extinct. At this epoch in Egypt (and there can be no doubt as we get a full record of this stage in the life of other early

societies we shall see the same thing taking place)
we can then watch civilisation going through a
critical but inevitable phase, illustrative and pro-
jective, as are all such crises, of a crisis in the spirit
of man. For this Ritual Killing of the King, though
it does not last long, marks a very important phase
in the growth of man's mind and its social consciousness. Before that phase he has always been directly
conscious of the tribe as a whole and therefore of its
eternal life and of his and his generation's identity
with it. He therefore does not need to focus his sense
of the group on a person. Loyalty is as impossible a
notion for him as for us is altruism toward our body.
So there is no need for one person to act as go-
between and conductor between extant individuals
and the reservoir of potential racial life – at such a
later stage conceived as lying 'beyond.' Every one
is the tribe and the tribe is eternal. It is in the
transitional period between this time of direct and
dominant group sense, and the time when the
individual will have established himself as the End
of the community (instead of the community being
the End of the individual) that we get the Ritual
Killings of the King. The gradual transformation
of these from Murders to Mummings is an exact
indication of the gradual emergence of the individual's sense of his sole importance.

Thus even the ritual classic phase, each time that
it reasserts itself, is not a blind and hopeless retrogres-
sion. It is consolidation and co-ordination. During

this time reflection grows, a mass of new and incoherent factual experience is made self-consistent and agreeable with authority. So the third and Fourth Dynasties are foundational. This age has at its beginning the Tomb of Zozer the Holy, fossilisation of the common life of his day. At its end it has the hypertrophied growth of the Pyramids. Cheops builds a monument which is not monstrous merely because of its size but because of its finish. This mountain of quarried stone is fashioned to the heart with the precision of watchmakers' work, every joint being fitted with a meticulous care that only a sense of its supreme magical significance could have ensured. Here are the patient accuracy, perfect focus and complete technique that could make instruments of scientific precision, employed to make an artificial mountain to a simple mathematical design. So we may gauge the energy pent in Egypt at the end of its most classic period.

When we watch the ape and even the savage and see how wayward, incoherent and diffuse is their mental energy, and then look at the Great Pyramid, we have not only an indication of how much force the new society had been able to accumulate but some criterion as to how long that Society could last before all that power of persistent effort was exhausted and the nation was psychically bankrupt.

Perhaps we may say that the power of an early society to endure may be gauged by the size of the holy works it can execute during its classic period, its period of co-ordination. Of these works made by other societies in other lands we have nothing approaching those of Egypt. Yet the Great Tels of Mesopotamia are still mighty landmarks, and such was the size of the greatest of these in its day that men thought Babel was built to touch the sky. And throughout the world there is no ancient site but it has its vast prehistoric works which have overawed the more fugitive, febrile and individualised peoples that have followed. 'These,' said the vagrant conquerors, 'are the works of gods or giants.' And truly they were works beyond the power of men of action. 'These,' said the rationalists, 'are the works of wretched slaves, innumerable toiling masses under the taskmaster's whip.' Individualism could not conceive such work being done save under such compulsion. But no whip could have made the stones of the Great Pyramid to fit with such precision. The compulsion that made that work was a spell, an urge of magic, and the power so to persist comes just at that moment when energy is at the highest pitch it can attain without bursting the old bounds and flooding out into unbounded explorations and indefinite inventions. The great works are then the high tide mark of the great age of accumulation. The great works, like the Ritual Killing of the King, mark a very definite epoch in the emergence of man. They must therefore give rise to and end in another and greater age of expansion.

V

The classic phase leads however, because of the completeness of its success, to a temporary exhaustion. This is not so much an exhaustion of the will as of the ideas on which the will has worked. Men are not in despair but in confusion of mind. They feel that the traditional canons no longer frame and shape their experiences. They fidget, they obstruct, they break out. And so in between the Classic and the Romantic Phases, there is a short phase of shaking loose – an age of disorder.

When a great body of water breaks its banks there is a time when the full flood has yet to carve its way and, in a confusion of water and earth, the passage is being opened. So the Sixth Dynasty is one of uncertain development. Pyramids are still being built, but with no sense of the real significance. The work is poor, the joints patched, the centres filled with rubble. The work is not a work of magic. It is no more than an archaistic copy of something the informing spirit of which is no longer understood. These Pyramids are the outward and visible sign of a change in the spirit of man. They are made because tradition, no longer understood, makes this arbitrary demand. The people of the Sixth Dynasty honoured their religion with their hands, but their heart was far from it. The past was no longer living in them.[1]

---

[1] We have seen it was in this Dynasty that the ritual killing of Pharaoh had sunk to a sham.

There follows, therefore, another age of expansion, and religion and magic must carry on as well as they may. The real worth of life is again in adventure and the future, not in conservation and contact with the sacred past. And of this change in man we can see clear traces in their religion. As long as man reverences the living past there is an eternal present keeping pace with him. And the future? – it hardly concerns him. It hardly matters to enquire what happens to the individual soul. It lives in the hands of the eternal Life. Its frontiers are within that, that is known; for the rest, its own exact limits are an arbitrary division, never certain now, so how speculate what they will be hereafter? Therefore it is only necessary to speculate about the life of the Pharaoh. If he is eternal then all the rest is deathless. In the old Kingdom, therefore, the Pharaoh alone has a clearly described future life. The passage of his spirit into the other world is delineated because he goes there as the father of his people, as their quintessential nature – he is their soul. And the world he goes to is not far and alien. It is near: in fact, not farther than go the roots of the crops. For he, whether manifest on the throne or potential in the tomb, is always in touch with the upper and lower world making a unity of life, keeping going the circulation of the double system, over the threshold. He is not merely Pontifex but Pons, the bridge and gate of life. But as he and his people become more active and enterprising, and their adventures lead them afield, they grow out of touch with the sacred spots and the simple cycle. The realm of death becomes a strange and vast place, instead of an intimate and fecund level just underfoot. As while in the body it had become an adventurer, now out of the body it wanders lonely into trackless spaces an unguided, unwanted pioneer.

Such a notion, we can now see, inevitably follows on a life of action. The Hero becomes the first survivalist. Nor is the social rot confined to him. It must spread to all who follow him. So personal survival becomes a live issue. Such self-centredness, which was quite new, is the gravest peril that can threaten a community. The attacks of enemies and the failure of its crops may only consolidate a group and make it resolve more desperately to hold together and resist to the bitter end. But the inner attack, the cold paralysis of doubt, the self-centred egotistic disintegration of individualism, against this there is no natural glowing reaction. It may therefore have been no disadvantage but a great help that at the time when personal survival after death first began to be a problem among the upper classes, the whole community was suddenly threatened by a great danger from without. To understand this we must recall, as mentioned above, that while certain groups of early men had come down from the plains into the river valleys there to found villages, others had still clung to the pastures. There, with a growing dominance over the flocks they followed, they

specialised into the nomad. For some time they lived
in this way with growing prosperity. But Nature was
against them and they were doing nothing to make
themselves independent of Nature: they were an
atavism, and therefore their only future must be
rigid conservatism or parasitism. The progressive
dessication caused by the moving north of the rain
belt and by the drying up of the glacier fed rivers,
that dessication which had provoked the first
civilisations, by sending men down into the river
valleys to become agriculturists, now threatens
those civilisations, by sending after the pioneers
these nomad laggards. The first 'barbarian invasions' seem to have struck down on the first civilisations about the time when these civilisations had
already advanced dangerously far in speculation.
In successive waves the grass lands were emptied on
to the valleys. There must have been many such
waves. We have historical record of several of them.
About 2000 B.C. came one, another about 1200, and
a third about 700. But before all these the human
deluge from the steppe had become part of the
phase of civilisation. We shall have to wait until we
learn from fuller excavation which of these repeated
descents destroyed the Indus proto-civilisation. That
of the Mesopotamian valley faced 'The Men of
Gutium who knew no Kings,' and though many of
the little cities were smashed, the Gu themselves
settled in the valley and took on most of its culture
until in a few generations they disappeared. Civilisa-

tion assimilated its attacks. In Egypt also the continuity, though distorted, was not terminated. A flood descended, drove itself in among the nation in the valley, but was soon again blended, as the waters of the Blue Nile descending into the White for a time would seem to wish to hold part of the river bed for itself, but after a little while there is but one water, a single flood made mightier by the addition.

But such invasions were not merely passively sustained and overcome by the civilisations. The invaded learned also from the invader. If the nomad would use organised raiding so as to save himself from starvation why should not civilisation counter-raid him to save itself the labour of agriculture? So after the victory of civilisation over the temporarily dominant nomads, civilisation does not go back to where it had been before the raid. The interaction, the fusing of the pastoralist with the agriculturist leads to a new step up in self-consciousness. The effort of repelling and assimilating led to a testing of traditions. Men's minds were also invaded and made receptive and capable of enquiry. Some of the old forms were abandoned. But on the whole men made their lives more complicated – they did not tend at this stage to simplify and puritanise them. That was to come later. Both sides, in this re-blending of these two streams of mankind, had traditions able to be and worthy of being combined. The nomads had become worshippers of the idea of unity (germ of the concept of law) and their symbol was that which undoubtedly, in the emptiness of the uplands, had suggested the unity of all, the Sun. So we see the sun religion, which till then was weak among the agriculturists and always tending to be choked in the fecund polytheism of the valleys, suddenly strengthened. Hathor, the cow goddess in Egypt, now has the sun between her horns. The tilled and teeming earth is linked with the pure sky. Hammurabi (*circa* 2000 B.C.), the great conqueror who combines Sumer and Akkad into a single land, gives a code of intense civic complexity, but he receives it from the Sun – its sanctioner is the God of the nomad man. On the other hand Pharaoh, now a warrior, continues, nevertheless, only able to inherit the throne of Egypt, not through his arms but through his wife, and his coronation was not valid until the marriage was consummated. While in Mesopotamia in the Holy of Holies at the top of each great Tower of Babel or Ziggurat, there was no altar, no Holy Table, but only a Holy Bed. So we may say we have a concordat – a coming together and a blend of two human traditions – the one of the plain and the other of the valley. War is now somewhat more definite and distinct a thing, more realist we should say. Men are more conscious that they enforce by use of physical violence and less by magic. To that degree they are more individual, less community-minded. But war now is not war for war's sake. The turbulence and love of fighting of the nomad has been canalised and made to defend, even if it weigh down, civilisation. The warrior king who appeals to the Sun God to be judge between the complex claims of his business subjects uses weapons to guard rather than to loot culture. The goose that lays golden eggs may be cooped but it is not killed.

Yet this settlement is not a permanent platform on which man may abide for ever. It is only a step. If the danger from the nomads were all civilisation had to fear it would now be safe. What it has to fear is, however, something far deeper – the continued emergence and intensification of the Spirit of Man: the unavoidable growth of individuality and self-consciousness. So the State must elaborate and disintegrate, and so the appeal to force must grow, because the belief in magic wanes. Yet the failure of the belief in magic is really proof, to those who can see, that the attempt to build on violence must be doomed to even speedier collapse.

CHAPTER IV

THE DAWN OF INDIVIDUALITY

I

Up to this point a single story has been told. The
clue of man's history has had many actual strands,
but through all these local varieties we can see the
same fate is being spun – for fundamentally the
same problems are being faced and are being solved
by minds fundamentally the same. Even when the
story is being carried on in three distant places, in

the Indus Valley, that of Mesopotamia and that of the Nile, we see it is the same story told in various dialects and easily interpretable, because, whatever the speech, it is dealing with and points to concrete things. But as civilisation grows, the simple themes become lost under the complexities of the orchestration. It is not merely that we ourselves are closer to the origin of the music. It is that the music itself is more complicated. Civilisation is the increase of variety, the increase of distinctions. We can no longer be sure that a phrase or a concept, even though it seem to be concrete, has behind it, and is based on a concrete object. This loss of concreteness, of a backing of fact, this emergence of pure ideas adds greatly to the task of interpretation. The first stages of civilisation are mainly increases in 'materials,' in quantity. Man makes fresh finds, but nearly all the advances in his mind are marked and made distinct by resultant advances in his power over the outer world. We can trace the growth of his mind by the growth of his gear and his works. This gear and these works are often curiously limited, but there they are, definite, concrete. We wonder why he so confined himself and restricted his achievement: why he paid such heavy tribute to the imaginary: but we feel that his aim, however handicapped, was always directed to the mastery of the external world and we assume that, as soon as he became sufficiently free of superstition, he must have become wholly devoted to a perfectly efficient exercise of his material powers. The fully civilised would be the fully materialised. The failure of man, as he advanced in civilisation, to attain such a materialism so puzzled the rationalists of the nineteenth century that they could only assume the failure to be due to wickedness. Certain people at the head must have seen that the advance of mankind toward complete efficiency must mean their elimination. Therefore they conspired to make the ordinary man believe that he could not be materially successful without their magical aid. Such conspiracies have, however, never been disclosed in history and it is growing ever more certain that they never took place, any more than that fancied primal contract that set the first king over an originally free people. What we do see (but what until this rationalisation of the conspiracy of the few and the martyrdom of the many was removed, could not be understood) is that it is the very people at the top, 'the exploiters,' who are the first to develop, explore and even become imprisoned by the immaterial. Early man is neither a materialist nor a spiritualist – he is a monist. One of the great turning points in history is therefore when Dualism appears. It becomes visible, naturally first to the advanced, and, as naturally, when they have to choose between matter and spirit, the dead and the alive, the world of means and quantity and the world of ends and quality, being human they cannot help but choose the human side. So the advances in civilisation that we have now to trace are most difficult to detect, because they are non-precipitant. It is true that man will make further great physical discoveries and will alter the world's face more in the modern age than during all the rest of the æon during which he has been man. Nevertheless it is true that his progress in this direction is very small in comparison with what it might have been, and the reason for that disparity is that the energy of his spirit has been divided and the main part has gone not into the understanding and mastery of the outer world but the exploration and experience of the inner. The discovery and exploration of his soul has divided his attention and so (and this is perhaps the most significant discovery of our day) he has only advanced in his knowledge of the outer world as he could win an equal and complementary knowledge of the inner. This fact will be seen to be of greater and greater importance as we continue to trace the upper stages of man's emergence.

But will not this growing dominance of ideas, this increasing absorption with abstractions, make the task of describing objectively what actually happened almost impossible? The elder historians dismissed man's psychological history as simply insignificant superstition. Our psychological age cannot do that. We cannot fail to recognise that the secret of man's growth lies there. But can we decode it? We must try. At least one thing helps us. That is that we do find that, though the course of history is now increasingly shaped by abstractions, it is the same set of abstractions that influence men's minds in whatever country they may live, so long as they have reached the same level of development. As, therefore, we continue to trace the same record, the Egyptian, because it is best preserved, we can continue to feel assured that it gives us in outline the history of an experience which all other civilisations as they reached each stage went through in their parallel advance. Therefore when trying to compose a picture that will illustrate this crisis in man's emergence, we may from a composition made out of the copious fragments it left in Egypt, form an idea of what must have taken place, under varieties of local form, in the history of all the other parallel civilisations, and also find the best, because the fullest, clues as to what was the fundamental and common force that underlay and informed this world-wide revolution. And historical opinion has of late come to a pretty general agreement that, at least as far as Egypt is concerned, the reign of Aknaton, at the close of the Eighteenth Dynasty, marks a crisis in the history of that civilisation and its entry on to a new way of life and a new vision of the universe. If humanity is one, we shall find similar thresholds marking the entry into a new age in the history of Mesopotamia, India and China. At present they are not known, so we must confine our attention to Egypt whose record alone approaches completeness. But here it must be repeated that it cannot be conceived that the other branches of human society omitted this important stage. Indeed, it seems impossible any longer to reject the belief that every important step in the advance in civilisation was repeated in all the world-wide variants of man's common fundamental culture. To say as much as this is not, however, to commit this sketch of history either to the belief of Diffusionism – that all cultures, ideas and forms are exported from Egypt on to a blank but receptive humanity – or to the opposite belief that human minds and societies all work like synchronised clocks striking all over the world the same chime at the same moment. The present writer is inclined to think the truth may lie between these two extremes and that what actually happened was that one society advancing ahead of the others in the common pursuit of well being and the common destiny of psycho-physical growth, such a society, at one time Egypt – at a later Judea – later again Greece – came to a dividing of the ways, made choice, found a solution and went ahead. Shortly after the other societies all arrived at the same point. Faced with the same problem and with the same capacities, it is not surprising that they sought about in the same way for a solution. The ancient world was far more in contact than we have imagined. Archæology leaves no doubt of that. It is agriculture that fastens man down. The food gatherer, the nomad, the merchant, in an unbroken succession have kept the cultures of the world from the Atlantic to the Pacific in touch since civilisation dawned. So when the various cultures reached at various times the same crisis, it would not be long before they learnt of the way in which the pioneer society – whichever it might be – had attempted solution. They were like patients comparing common symptoms and discussing their various treatments. They would not have to take over from one diffusing centre problem and solution, question and answer. The question was theirs and the answer of another branch of humanity would suggest the sense, though not necessarily the form, of their reply. Every devout thinker as he heard of another nation's religious crisis, must have prophesied in his spirit the words: 'Their Gods are as the Fates assign – their prayer, and all the world's, is mine.'

II

The life of Aknaton is therefore of world historical importance, because, as has been well said, he is the first individual in history. To say that there were many individuals before and that only the chance completeness of his record makes the Heretic Pharaoh stand out as a fully detached personality is really to rationalise the situation. Such a complete individual emerged, made his impress and left his emphatic record because he was the first complete person to be entirely precipitated. 'There may be many more lying lost in the night.' That is a natural

115

assumption for individualists to make, but it is an assumption. If we do not make that, if on the other hand we allow full weight to the fact against which our individuality irrationally fights, the fact that the individual is not the isolated unit that he assumes he is, that he is a resultant of a peculiar state of human society, then we shall see there is less and less reason to challenge Aknaton's right to be a lonely pioneer. For the detached individual is an abstraction. No person even in to-day's late condition of civilisation lives as a complete person save by drawing constantly upon one or the other of his social heredities. He may to-day have choice on which foundation he will stand, but on one, stand he must. He can no more be detached psychically from such a connective series than he can as a physical body float in air. If ancient society, prior to Aknaton, had no place for fully self-conscious, independent, eclectic individuality, then such an individuality, though it might bud and peep, could never break and emerge. No more than the sky in winter can rain roses, but slow grown stock and steadily warming weather must lead up to flowering, can a complete self-conscious individual appear in the close-shut unit of an early group. The first individual is therefore significant of much more than he knows, and his achievement is far greater than his acts. He will have new theories about the Universe and the soul's relation to it – these things he must have. He will strive to alter life so that it may be consonant with such theories. He will awake bitter opposition. His theories seem arbitrary: his acts futile. But unfounded speculation and defeated action are only symptoms. The real underlying fact, the fact of permanent value and of significance to the whole of life, is that the self-conscious, eclectic individual has appeared. Nor is it accident that he appears as a King. Only at the top can the tree of life begin to flower. Nor is the dynastic place of this individual king any more an accident than the fact that he is and must be a king. He comes at the close of a magnificent Dynasty, a Dynasty that recapitulated all the greatness of past ages and went beyond. The founder of the Dynasty Ahmosi breaks the Hyksos power and captures their great horde-camp at Avaris from which they had held down the country. This 'liberation' is followed by a series of mighty raids. Thetmosis I (1540 B.C.) behaves like a typical hero in his campaigns. But being no free lance of the uplands but Pharaoh of a revived Egypt he is something more than a hero in his policy. His elder sons being dead he takes the original and significant step of associating with him his very remarkable daughter on the throne. At his death this woman, Hatshepsut, ruled with her husband, Thetmosis II, but he is soon gone – a fleeting shadow that leaves her alone regnant. The national effort that she focuses and directs now begins to take on in full its unprecedented character. For not only are large extra-Egyptian territories now beginning to be permanently held, organised and integrated in a single policy, but definite exploration is undertaken. After simple war comes not only consolidation but also new ways of expansion. The land of Puoni or Punt is visited by an 'economic embassy.' Its chief yield is incense. The requirements of the gods are growing with the growth of men's wealth. But Egypt desires also a variety of luxuries. Raw power and plenty are not enough. Variety, curious stuffs, rare materials, strange beasts – all these are in demand. The mere catalogue of the Punt yield shows that in Egypt a speculative, fanciful mind has appeared. It is no longer horrified by the strange, but demands it with increasing appetite. It is therefore no surprise to find that the power which is directing this exploration of the unknown and this discovery of the curious is not a man. For this phase of Egyptian enterprise is directed and expressed by the sole rule of this Hatshepsut, the Virago. Manhood had made, even in Egypt, the crown a secondary male characteristic, for only a fighter could expand a nation, and magical peace, the spellbound stability of the completely suggestible group, had vanished with the matriarchy. Yet though the simple fighter must be pure male, once the short preliminary phase of simple fighting was past, then a mixture of strength and guile was better suited to carry on than simple strength. The trouble of pure strength is that it makes its possessor to depend purely on it. Yet so little is the strength of a man, compared with his cunning, that such dependence must be more fatal than absolute weakness. So a virago, a creature who could play the man – for Hatshepsut dressed herself partly as a man – but who yet was at heart acting – warily watching the effect of force, never unaware of how the strongest are often the stupidest and how a wild beast may remain helpless in a cage of laths – such a ruler is the natural expression and focus of Egypt's mind and achievement in the sixteenth century B.C. Even her dress illuminates her place and person. The Egyptians shaved the body all over. That one reason for this may have been cleanliness, only explains the custom in so far that reason is considered sufficient to account for conduct – an explanation which our age realises does not go very deep. The Assyrians, who later raised a civilisation almost as elaborate and quite as rich, in an area where heat, insects and parasites made bodily cleanliness not less important, these mighty fighters and hunters and splendid persons gloried in their hair and with oil and comb made it an enlargement of their person. There is every reason to suppose that they kept their prized bodies as clean as did the Egyptian. All that we see points to the fact that they must have thought even more about their bodies and specifically of their maleness. The Egyptian cleanliness was therefore probably only a by-product of a profounder purpose. Had they not desired to minimise the difference of the sexes they would have found, like the Assyrians, some way of keeping their hair clean without cutting it all off. Hair is the most important of the secondary sexual characteristics. The insult of the shaven beard rings through the Heroic Age. Is not the eunuch marked to all eyes by his beardlessness? Swears not the last of the heroic nomads by the Beard of his Prophet? No, the beardlessness of Pharaoh is of profound psychosocial significance. Shaving is as profound a revolution as we have seen was the tattoo. The tattoo was the mark whereby man, at once on the outer body and by sharp sensation in the feelings, discovered and deliminated the frontier between himself and the outer world. The shave was the next great step. But as the tattoo was to mark himself off from the continuum around, the shave was to see how close, because he wished to be a social unit more than a family man, he could come to being not a mere male but a human being. Nature had so marked out the sexes but the mark was not ineradicable. Men and women in Egypt soon realised that what they had in common, their minds and their skill of hand or tongue were far greater than their differences. The ideas that lead to matriarchy, it would seem, were never here completely extirpated, and so the division between male and female was never permitted to spread from its sexual province and invade social life. There was a phase when the Hero was dominant, but he never succeeded in rooting up the people from the land. So magic and social ties rather than physical power and military success are what preserve Egypt throughout. It must have been during an outburst of maleness, when the heroic leader was trying to break with the tradition of priestly dominance (that kept a Pharaoh as tied as though he were a matriarch herself) that the beard was made part of the royal insignia. Yet it was but as part of the royal insignia that it was worn. It was as little part of the person, it was as much part of the office, as was the rest of the regalia – the agricultural sceptres – the magic flail and crook – the towering complex of the double mitre – for the beard was as detachable as they. It was a sham beard – a detachable vestment of ritual, as much as the great necklaces and the asp-serified sandals. Indeed, long before the date we have reached in this sketch, the Eighteenth Dynasty, it has ceased to be even a convincing sham. It is no longer a pretence beard but merely a symbol for royalty, a piece of wood conventionally shaped, attached to the chin by strings about the ears. It was no more to be taken for a beard than to-day are spectacles taken for eyes. It was this mark of rank, then, that Hatshepsut adopted, not to become a man and so disguised to hold the throne, but to show that a woman could put on the full majesty of the state. Though she wears the insignia of royalty, even when this insignia has been derived from secondary male characteristics, that she was claiming an office and not pretending a sex is proved by her inscriptions in which she does not speak of herself in the male but in the female gender. And her achievement leaves no doubt that she also showed that the State had now reached such a phase in its development that its expression and focus could not be a purely male creature of action; but that the ruler, whether physiologically male or female, must combine in his or her spirit, with resolution cunning, with action reflection, with executive ability speculation, with formality and conformity, a cynical perception of their formalism, and yet, not less, with the exercise of force and violence an equally cool realisation of *their* limits and of the counter-vailing strength of tradition, suggestion, habit and reverence. That this virago possessed all these qualities we may be sure, for it is not merely her external achievement that shows her so to have been possessed. For not only did she explore the land of Punt, not only did she worthily follow and develop the expansions of her mighty father; all the while she had to hold in check the growing ambition of seed royal as potent as the stock from which it sprang. For Hatshepsut had a constant rival at her side. Her husband-brother Thetmosis II had had by a concubine a son whom he had wished to reign, but whom the Queen, when she took the throne, had put aside. He had, however, inherited the genius of the family. Yet till the day of her death she kept him helpless. What an achievement that was we may judge by the heroic exploits he, when free of her, achieved. And of the constant vigilance she must have exercised to keep him helpless we can also judge when we see the discharge of hatred with which he overthrew all her memorials and expunged everywhere her detested name.

In passing, as we look at Egypt's monuments and recognise the passion that possessed this people to be remembered, we must surely recognise a vivid illustration of the psychological problem: why is it that a creature which by its continual recording of its evanescent features in harder and harder material shows how it recognises its own evanescence and its dependence on the charity of posterity, why should such a creature strive to assert itself by boast and display? The one must awake the wish to deny and the other to deface. After all, it may be that, in literal truth – the only enduring memorial is to have been self-forgetful, and that here, too, the hedonistic paradox may extend and the only eternal life may be for those who have ceased to pursue it or to desire. Certain it is that the dynastic energy passed its climax with the death of Thetmosis III. As long as the sister-repressed general can feel her hated shadow behind him so long must he strive to go ever further to get outside its abominable bound. She had understood the power of peace, building up the temples at home and abroad, developing trade and diplomacy. He would, in contrast, specialise in warfare, and we read in the detail with which he records his campaigns not only a new objective attitude to war, the rise of specific strategy, of troops handled as single units and manœuvred with a complete freedom from both the simple fighting of individuals and the working of group magic, but also of a mind dominated by the delight of the new game – a game in which a man's will may have full expression with a man's mind and all feminine shifts of diplomacy have an end. His successors, Amenophis II and Thetmosis IV, try and repeat his achievements, but are without his driving power.

III

Then comes the next phase with Amenophis III. He has to fight but his heart is not in it. He is on the defensive. He quells revolt but he wants to leave war alone. He seems to have seen no sense in such ardours. Increasingly he settled down to enjoy. Here found he himself placed on the top of a heap of looted riches such as no man had ever seen before, let alone possessed. Why strive for more? Here was more than a man in all his all too short lifetime could enjoy or even handle. So possessed, so overwhelmed, so suffocated with plenty it was a struggle just to live. The human soul for the first time emerged on to the new higher level of Natural Selection, the Natural Selection no longer through the body but that more exact Selection through the mind. In comparison with that, the older form was really simpler. The will to live, even when it is no more than a spark, is more often blown to a flame by the winds of hardship and misfortune than it is blown out. Those which are so extinguished are completely put out and what remains burns with a clear intense flame of conviction that life is supremely with the living. But with plenty, the flame can be choked, desire can fail, the links become unlocked, the appetite may turn to nausea. It was this, the next phase of Natural Selection, the phase which concerns increasingly the whole of modern society, the phase we are doing so little to prepare against, which is the phase we can see dawning on the lonely Pharaoh who was raised 3400 years ago to such a height of plenty, to such a limitation and restriction of every ordinary aim through unlimited means, that unless he could find extra human interests he must die of psychic inanition. We know he lived on. We know he took to the usual atavistic exercise with which the rich unemployed always attempt to escape from the emptiness of their lives – he was a great hunter and slew many lions. He also attempted to use his great powers by competing with Nature, for he made a great artificial lake; otherwise he seems to have tried to content himself with passive possession. He found no new way of using the new plenty which had been put at his disposal. He could not take and hold the initiative against this avalanche of plenty. He was a captive of others' conquests. He was immobilised in the relics and by-products of their excessive activity. He initiated no new science and the art of his period is the art of the over rich who try to excuse pettiness of design by costliness of material. The only opening for one debarred from action, whose every spontaneous appetite was stifled by surfeit before it could draw one full deep breath of keen desire, was an opening upward into acuter understanding and even more detached interest. This is the real strain of psychic Natural Selection. Can we make ourselves new appetites when the original spontaneous ones that kept life going have been built up and staunched at their sources? The present writer believes that such a Selection is even more drastic than the elder form. This is the newer, keener, more exhausting struggle for existence. Those that fail in it will increasingly take refuge from life's remorseless demand that they should live, in voluntary death. It also seems clear that when man emerges on this bleak plateau swept with the 'Trade winds that cross it from Eternity,' only the most resolute determination to plunge forward can save him. To-day tens of thousands have emerged on that plateau whence the outlook reveals only the stars. Only Science as a philosophy can make man able to take that step.

Amenhetep III lived and died. We know from his body that he lived to suffer toothache which his ignorant comforts could not cure and to be crippled with rheumatic disease. But, though he died without scandal, if not without horror, with honour if without achievement or hope, a harder fate was not

to be escaped by his heir. For his heir is Amenophis
IV, who was to call himself Aknaton and to be
branded as the blasphemer. So we see this unhappy
being set in his inevitable place; so we see why he
was the first individual. Action, discovery, enterprise, accumulation, ever more thought and originality to meet the unfamiliar that the early steps
of enterprise had revealed, these are the steps that
lead, without a break, to speculation about the very
basis of being and a resolve to dare to remodel the
whole of mankind's entire attitude to life. It is not
merely the murderer, the usurping Macbeth who
has, inevitably, in his effort to free himself from the
deed, to sink ever deeper in its whirlpool eddies. All
action swallows up the actor. Nor is withdrawal
possible. The only freedom is for the spirit to make
with all resolution along the path which it is being
drawn and, casting aside the self as a limitation, to
pursue, faster than it can retreat, the mysterious
desire which has beckoned it. That desire, Proteus-
like, will change its form, but as the revealing myth
relates, if, disregarding his own safety, caring only
for the object, man holds to it, it will finally tell him
all, both what it is and what he is. Aknaton as
individual and as autocrat was inevitable. His
individuality and his autocracy were interdepen-
dent. The one could not have been complete without
the other. He is therefore compelled to attempt to
impose universally what is inevitably an individual
outlook. So he is addressed to cataclysm. The time

will come when others will attain the station which at his time he had solitarily to occupy. But that time is not for some eight hundred years. Meanwhile as autocrat-individualist, as the man of lonely conscience, through comprehensive power he must fulfil his destiny and, though master of the world, come to realise that he is more a stranger and an outcast in it than his lowliest fellaheen. For they all had place; he alone had been called to go out into spiritual banishment. The acts of Aknaton need not be described. His whole effort was to break with tradition and to replace the authorised religious amalgam, in which at that stage sun worship was entangled with Fertility rites, by a religion in which the worship of the sun should be exclusive of all other cults. The form of this controversy seems arbitrary. Did not the priesthood worship predominantly Amon Ra, the sun? Why make a revolution to assert a priority which was undoubtedly gradually asserting itself? Was not the real meaning of this struggle that the king wished to win from the priesthood their power, and thought, by denying their dogma, to shatter their authority? Such an explanation is too simple. The form this controversy took is significant. The worship of the sun, we have seen, is in the succession of worships, a late one. There must have been an æon of diffused, rudimentary worship before the moon gathered to itself the reverence as the Queen of Heaven. The moon in its turn must have reigned for long before the sun began to displace her. In fact, it seems increasingly clear that sun worship does not and cannot arise until man can have such foresight and deductive power that he can foresee the whole cycle of the year and deduce the process of the seasons from the presence and station of the Sun. When man has attained such foresight and deductive power he has become an individual, for not only is he capable of considerable ratiocination but, even more decisive, he can conceive time and, therefore, of himself as a constant unit moving through it.

Sun-worship therefore marks, as we have seen the rise of the nomads, the enterprising hero-led individuals who diverged from the stable group-tradition and took to a life of exploration, initiative and adventure. We have seen also that as the sun-worship came among the early agriculturalists of the Nile Valley it made its way by a syncretism with the earliest totemism.[1] For this alliance was naturally selected the hawk (or falcon), the one animal that seems to go near the sun, and the great Temple of Amon Ra – the Sun – has as its symbol the hawk. Now with Aknaton we see the same process of individualising attained, not in the break away and tradition-cleared air of the desert, but actually in the very labyrinth of religion. Here, therefore, the effort had to be greater. The nomad could make a

[1] Hathor the Cow first has the moon between her horns and then the sun. This illustrates the way her agricultural worshippers slowly identified their farm totem with larger conceptions of the sky.

physical break away, and being able to escape and to continue on the move he not only was rid of the task of having to counter the objections of conservatives. Having flung out, he continued to have his fling. He did not ponder the drive that was in him. He vented his balked feeling in movement, and never speculated why it was obvious to him that the single god of the sun was the one true God and why it was therefore right for him to destroy the fat and fertile idolators. But Aknaton becoming an individual in the heart of a complete society had to become a theologian of the sun, to explain, if only to himself, the changed attitude toward worship, which was really awoken by his new individual self-consciousness. He spends his power in trying to extirpate the polytheism, and plant his monotheism in its place. All the old totem gods must go. Only that one, Horus the hawk, is spared in the great temple of Amon Ra because he is associated with and symbol of the Sun.

Aknaton's failure is as inevitable as his emergence. On every tree there must be a first flower and it must be cast before the general flowering. Again, it must be noted that if we could know the history of the great branches of man's tree – the Chinese, the Indian, and the Mesopotamian – as well as we know the Egyptian, we then should be able to detect this 'individualising out' at the top, in the three others, as we can in this the one whose complete record alone we have. Certain it is, when we reach the time when

the tree has come to its time of general flowering,
that we find every branch is thick with the same
flowers.

The life of the heretic Pharaoh is therefore not a
futile tragedy. He was the first fruits of the resurrection of the spirit of man: he was the forerunner of a
new age. It has proved a cold world into which that
lonely individualised spirit has emerged, but man
could not sleep any longer. He was raised from his
slumber within the group and henceforward he
must go on until he can rise even further and see
himself and the group, from a higher standpoint,
again made one.

CHAPTER V

THE FIRST REFORMATION

THE history of the next six hundred years is a history
of increasing awareness. Man's power over the
outer world grows step by step as an answer to, a
projection of, the growth of his own self-conscious-

ness, the sense that he dare think for himself, question tradition, challenge authority, analyse the deposit of doctrine and select and combine with the specific purpose of satisfying his private aims. Under this strain society often collapses. Repeatedly Egypt disintegrates back to a feudal system, down to an anarchy. From the south the Nubians temporarily dominate a higher but distracted people. From the north comes, worse than the Hyksos, the descendant of the Shepherd King stock, the Semite Assyrians as savage as any barbarian but equipped with the instruments of war civilisation had invented. But Egypt either assimilates or expels. Her strength is submerged but not drowned. She re-emerges as the Sacred Land itself emerges, from the annual inundation, and society continues the inevitable evolution. Finally with such a Pharaoh as Psamtek (664-610 B.C.) we reach a culmination. Here is a king admirably efficient, for he builds up Egypt once again into a great power. He rallies the people and expels the savage Assyrians. But he is no mere soldier. Indeed he himself is sprung from specifically priestly stock. But though essentially a great church man and a man of action we know that he was possessed of a most speculative and original mind, for Herodotus had heard that it was he who, with an experimental enterprise worthy of a Greek, had sought to discover what was the primal speech of man. This he had done by having brought up in silence so many male and female children. Think of

the type of mind such experimentation reveals.
First it has speculated on origins. The able adminis-
trator dealing with many dialects found time to
speculate how they may have arisen. He looks down
time and has before his mind's eye æonic perspec-
tives. This is the first step to science. And he takes
the second as well. For he initiates experiments. He
envisages his problem and undertakes an investiga-
tion, the results of which he cannot hope to see for
some years. Surely this is the second stage of the
individual, of the growth of self-consciousness and
the emergence of modern man. Here is no longer a
distracted visionary misunderstanding himself and
trying with futile fanaticism to impose the rationalisation and projection of his own abnormal mental
condition on a society that had not attained to his
condition and which, when it should attain that
condition, could not be assuaged by such a projection. On the contrary, instead of the decadent
descendant of a terrific line, squandering the power
which he never could have won, we have a resourceful statesman who built up his country, by his
knowledge of its limitations and powers, and by the
exercise of such originality that, in the task of the
consolidation of a new order, he still had time to
speculate about the past and how it was that the
present had come about. We are not surprised to
learn that this king has many Greeks at his court,
and his forces include Greek and other alien
mercenaries.

Yet the course of the evolution of man's mind and thought, the full emergence of man did not run smooth. Even the little calm into which the Saite Dynasty seemed to have steered Egypt, did not last. They freed the land from the Assyrians and gave the people for a short time a new rule suited to that new day. It was, however, only a sunny space between two storms, for the very flood that had finally overwhelmed Assyria, the Persian power, shortly after swamped down into Egypt, and the country's independence was gone. And had there been political continuity it is doubtful whether the whole of society could have followed the spiritual evolution of its leaders without revolution. Certain it is that the fact that it had been shown that kings could become philosophers did not save the ordinary man, when his turn came, from having to begin again where the kings had begun, and for the subject to have to go through a heretic phase, as had the Ruler. Indeed, it was as Psamtek was making the first scientific experiments that the first individuals were beginning to emerge in embarrassing numbers among the commonalty and to recapitulate, as far as in them lay, the behaviour of Aknaton. If the fifteenth century B.C. is the first day of man's earliest spring – the century in which the full individual first appears anywhere on the tree of life, the eighth century B.C. is a date not less important. For in this century individuals appeared so generally and in such numbers that religion, which the autocrat Pharaoh had tried in vain to alter in the direction of individuality, suddenly was transformed in that interest.

As it happens, we cannot trace that revolution directly in Egypt: perhaps the Pharaohs were too intelligent to give it occasion, and themselves introduced such alterations in divine service that the new dawning susceptibilities were soothed, if not satisfied. But we have a record of this uprising, and that we have so is perhaps not very miraculous. For we must remember that what we witness is a revolution in the mind of man whereby he became self-conscious and reflective. It is not surprising, therefore, that however much earlier phases may have gone unrecorded, this phase is amply documented. This is the dawning age of autobiography, of the soul's struggle set down, and preserved and conned by succeeding generations as in their souls' voyage they too had to take the course that these first pilots had charted.

Nor was it accident that Judea should be the area in which this revolution first broke out. The Hebrews had at this date, when they were settled around Jerusalem, a mixed social heredity. Two dominant strains were present. The first was the strain they had from Egyptian sources. This was the religion of Fertility. It worshipped the cow as its totem god and there was mixed with this comparatively advanced agricultural religion a ruder one whose sacred pillars were as crude in shape as they were frank in signification. The second strain, intruded on this, was a pastoral nomadic religion, the totem animal of which was naturally the lamb – the symbol of the nomad's flock against the village dweller's herds.[1] These pastoral nomads, as we have seen, are spontaneously monotheistic. They belong to a stage of mental evolution ahead of the agriculturalist still shut close in his conservative community and bound in the sanctified unvarying routine of his unchanging surroundings and invariable duties. There must therefore have been a jar when the two cultures blended and the blend must always have shown the mark where further cleavage would in time take place. But for some centuries there was an amalgam; as we have seen in more stable Egypt, the religion of sun and cow had made a syncretism. Then, in the eighth century B.C. in Palestine, trouble becomes apparent. For many generations there had existed, it would seem, bands of unstable men who roamed the country. These dervishes[2] may well have been relics of nomadry unassimilated, when the main invasion settled down and combined with the people of the land, and there is certainly reason to suppose that though they had become specifically religious they

---

[1] The cow cannot live on the short steppe herbage as can the sheep, as it plucks up the grass by winding its tongue round it and not by incising it close to the root; it must have lush valley meadow if it is to thrive.

[2] The early Hebrew word for prophet and mad fellow is the same, and still among such conservative Semites as the Arabs a mad man is protected as one inspired.

were not friendly to the ritualised religion. For it is their name that is taken by the first attackers of that religion. If we are to trust the present state of our records, the first prophets to become important, disregard the temple or temples and seek communion with spiritual power on sacred mountains. They also actively champion the sky father against the fertile phallic religion, and a war of extermination goes on between the adepts of either side. Then it would seem after a couple of generations in which the issue hung in the balance the champions of the sky father win. The earth religion is driven to concentrate itself on one centre. All the provincial shrines are suppressed, and only at Jerusalem may religion be practised. This victory was, however, only a step toward a sedan. The religion which was now confined to Jerusalem was still an amalgam. All was now in the name of a single deity, but that deity might still be worshipped both as the sky father of nomad individuals or as the principle of all plenty, the power of fertility. Such worship is the projection of a transitional mind. Not much longer would the Hebrew halt between two opinions. He must go on to full individuality, and that being so he must rid his religion of all racial significance. We have one of the actual documents with which the attack was launched. The first Hebrew prophet whose writings survive is the prophet Hosea, and this document we find is an attack on the immemorial rites of the national religion. The prophet is outraged that his wife has had to undergo at the Temple by the priestly surrogates of its god the fertilising which had always been considered essential if the marriage was to prove fruitful. Why does this man suddenly question authoritative tradition and why is his protest considered so right that men preserve it century after century? Surely we must own that this protest is produced by the same revolutionary mental condensation that produced the reforms of Aknaton. In both cases an individual must revolt against what to a pre-individual was right, satisfying, authoritative. From this time, therefore, there will grow up a new religion and a new morality. Indeed the old religion will be held to be immoral and detestable; as something to be extirpated. And though this new movement is so revolutionary and original, it will win. The old original religion will everywhere give way before it, and so complete will be the victory of the new that hardly a trace of the old will be left standing. That this is no fanciful interpretation of history can be seen from the judgment of such a scholar as Dr. Rhys Davis. 'Suddenly, and almost simultaneously, and *certainly independently*, there is evidence about the sixth century B.C. in each of these widely separated centres of civilisation (Nile, Euphrates, Ganges and Yellow River) of a leap forward in speculative thought, of a new birth in ethics, of a religion of conscience, threatening to take the place of those old religions of custom and magic' (*Buddhist India*).

THE EMERGENCE OF MAN

The only part of this judgment that the present writer would modify is that which holds the outbreak to have occurred spontaneously in the four great branches of human society. Exact dating seem to show that in Judea the first stirrings of the ethical prophetic movement began certainly not later than the middle of the ninth century, and Josiah, the reforming king, who puts into force the desires of the prophets (by killing the holy men and women in the Temple and setting up the law as the national morality) reigns in the seventh century. Though all the branches of the human tree may have been ready to bring forth this strange flower, the Jewish shoot certainly seems the first to have done so, and its example may quite possibly have become known to the rest.

But it may be asked, Even if this is so, even if in these centuries the human mind underwent an unprecedented revolution and human consciousness emerged into a completely new, more intense and more clear conception of itself and speculation as to its origin and end, all that is of interest to the historian of religion, but is it significant for history as a whole?

Let us then continue to trace the growth of civilisation. We see that the new 'moral' notions of the Hebrew prophets not only are indicative, are projections of, a new condensation and individualising of consciousness, but that these notions show themselves to be of universal appeal. In other words, wherever civilisation has reached a certain level there men inevitably find in themselves, in their consciousness, a new attitude to life and to the world. These ancient societies, filled with new men, are therefore about to undergo a transformation equal to the change that had taken place in the minds of their constituents. That this development was no whim of arbitrary prohibitionists we can judge by its success. In the Far East, Confucius can win royal support for his new morality whereby as the old cake of custom had melted he attempted to rebond the State with calculatingly moral individuals. Buddah in India gains influential support for the new morality, and, not long after, the royal genius Asoka deliberately adopts Buddism and expends much of his great State's resources in propagating the doctrine. At this date too it seems Zoroaster in Persia began the same 'individualising' of morality and religion and managed to enlist on its behalf the military genius that was in a few generations to make Persia a greater power than the world had so far seen.[1]

These were the reactions of society as a whole, of complete nations, to the revolutionary feeling, the sense of personal individuality that had awoken among the few at the top. In some cases we can catch sight, not of the amalgamator, not of the new spirit in full reaction with the old mass but of the pure spirit itself. Beside Confucius we catch sight of the mysterious figure of Lao Tze. Confucius aims

---

[1] See further, p. 183.

at reconciling the new individual and the old state
by sacrifices made by both of their extreme claims.
Lao Tze would seem to have stated simply and
completely the demands of the individual soul and
its sense of the worthlessness of all the social matrix
out of which it had crystallised.[1] So too Buddah
was not concerned himself with the problem as to
how the state was to carry on when it was composed
(or decomposed) of individuals. He spoke to the
individual and never hinted that the state had any
rights or power of control over him. 'Behold,' he
is said to have summed up his teaching, 'I show you
one thing; Sorrow and the ending of Sorrow.' He
preaches, naked and unashamed, the flight of every
conscious being out of society and the world.

The Hebrew prophets seem to have been less
doctrinaire: the early ones undoubtedly are con-
cordists. They wish to see the state modified to
accept the morality this new person, the individual,
must demand. They wish the erotic element (which
is really the racial element) to be taken out of
religion and they wish in social relations – which
developments in money have upset – a social self-
conscious contract between masters and men. But
behind their doctrines and their practical recom-
mendations is the ultimate feeling that the individual
is final and that if he is not satisfied, then society is
a failure and civilisation had better go to judgment.

[1] Cf. 'The trouble with the people is that there is so much government.' In all his aphorisms there is a complete contempt for the State.

CHAPTER VI

THE MONEY-MADE MEN

I

THIS then is the fundamental fact about man's
history, that his mind is an emerging mind and that
as he continues to explore the outer world he does
so because he is urged thereto by an advance in his
own self knowledge. The interaction of outer circumstances (which he has largely made) and inner
reflection, will therefore cause the complicated
pattern of civilisation, a pattern which age by age
will become more intricate. At its base, however,
it will always be directed by one thing only, man's

growing sense of what he is. That, fundamentally, all changes in man's circumstances are due to change in his character can well be illustrated by an example from this phase of his history. For it is at this time that man made the discovery of money. Many early writers on history imagined that man must always have had cash. Now we can see not only why that discovery was made comparatively lately but why it was made at a particular moment. As moon worship marks a specific phase of man's emergence, because the worship of the moon could only take on its complete significance when man had reached that degree of consciousness when he could grasp as a single time-unit the month: as the worship of the sun also had to wait for its full recognition until man could think in years: so money had to wait until man had mastered number and could live with abstractions. The power of abstraction marks a very definite stage in man's growth (did not Emerson say generalisation is the distinctly human characterisation and has not Dr. Spearman found the power to grasp associations and to select a wealth of impressions into a single meaning as the sign-royal of mind?). But like all man's advances it has great dangers, and into these, perhaps of necessity, man fell. The danger of being able to have an abstract concept of time undoubtedly has always imperilled civilisation almost as much as it has helped to make civilisation possible. We have seen that a rudimentary state of society was possible when men first saw as far and could live ahead as far as the month. Civilisation has been defined, by an author who has wished to describe it with a critic's eye for essentials, as the power to put off immediate satisfaction for future benefit. Those who could live a month ahead were more human than those who could not. So the moon civilisations have a distinct culture. They can accumulate commodities, and they can persist at tasks in a way the less foresighted cannot. But they can have only a very rudimentary culture and wealth. Agriculture is impossible without a concept of the year, without being able to look forward twelve months. Some sort of sun worship must therefore be the mark of fully agriculturised culture. So the sun culture would be far more powerful than the moon cultures. From thence we get such larger leases on the future as Olympiads and Lustra.[1] Men increasingly live in a state where the greater part of their acts refer to something non-existant, the future. But it is inevitable, we say; every to-morrow surely comes. No: one cannot say that if one is a realist. There is very little doubt that a to-morrow will come. But there is more and more doubt about every further morrow. Finally the very abstraction that teaches us that to-morrow must be

[1] It is significant that the first Olympiad, a four-year span, is dated 776 B.C. So we have another indication that about the eighth century ordinary men and not merely a priestly caste were able to 'hold in consciousness' as much as a tithe of their active life. The Roman Lustrum, a five-year span, is probably initiated a century later.

taken into account also teaches us that there is a to-morrow when we ourselves shall be of no more account. In fact, the power of time-abstraction shows itself, like all power, liable to the law of diminishing returns. Beyond a certain point it does not pay to plan – the Variables become too great. Beyond another point it is a positive loss to look, for there, one thing alone is certain – the planner will be no more. The supreme task of a civilisation, made up of individuals, is to find out where those points lie. Up to a point an individualised society can become increasingly powerful and efficient by the increase of the foresight of its individuals. Beyond that point their foresight may well prove fatal to it because the disparity, between their interest and its, becomes ever more irreconcilable. So man's first great abstraction, the abstraction of time, must at a certain point cease to be inevitably of social benefit and become a problem which it needs a completely new effort to solve.

Man's second great abstraction, the abstraction of power, depends of course on his abstraction of time. He could not attain to hoarding until he could look forward to lean seasons. No doubt like many other animals he had in his mental make-up a taste for storage, but it could not have been drawn out had not his sense of the future become clear in his consciousness. Yet another factor, beside an extended time sense, was needed before man could get beyond barter and invent money. That was an extension in space. His dealings had to do with peoples removed more than one degree, he had to do business through third parties and middle men. The hard black volcanic glass obsidian, which was found in the Greek islands, gives the finest cutting edge that man ever had, till he could forge steel. But it is brittle and so not of many uses; while employed for its few essential uses it may last for years. The obsidian market was therefore in the early world a very wide one and at the same time one that was easily 'flooded.' So we have two reasons why obsidian should be traded widely. There was a third as important. Obsidian tools are easily transported. That trade, therefore, in such small handy articles naturally flowed across many frontiers. And one of the places where it was found, the island of Melos, was situated as a natural 'bridge head' between a manufacturing area and a Europe of almost untouched raw materials. Would not therefore obsidian become the first money? No, because though hard, small, handy and uniform, it was too hard. You could not melt it nor could you cut it without great loss into standard bars. Those qualities belonged to metal. So silver is cast and cut and weighed, and silver is perhaps the first bullion. In several countries it has given its name to all money, and the pound is a name that recalls the fact that once the new gold pieces were rated to be equal to a pound of silver. But silver presents problems. When trading it by weight how should traffickers know that the bars they exchanged were standard? So coinage begins to appear. Metal takes a stamp well. The first coins are no more than metal weights on which the mark is really the assay stamp. But though stamped silver may be sterling in the market, it has disadvantages in store. Silver tarnishes easily and, long buried, may be completely corrupted. Hence a gold coinage is attempted for gold can endure. The first coins may well be the Lydian lumps of electrum. Nearby were mines which produced this metal – a mixture of gold and silver. Here at Sardis, the capital city, was naturally an exchange centre. For here two streams of civilisation met. On one side was the sea-traffic of the islands and coasts, the first spots where men could both be settled so as to manufacture and also free to hawk their wares. On the other side, on the East, were the first empires, building themselves up, with a demand for all the inventions and crafts of the first free artists and inventors.

So money precipitates naturally and, when present in one place, this new form of crystallised, pocketable power spreads rapidly through civilisation. As we have seen, it gravely deranges life. The early Hebrew prophets found themselves, the first reformers, not only up against what their new individual morality felt to be an outworn immoral religion but also up against a new immorality, money power.

The trader appeared, the speculator who with an

original foresight gambled on 'futures.' When he failed he was mocked and denounced as a mad innovator. When he succeeded he was as heartily denounced as a ruthless exploiter of the rightful source of all wealth, the husbandman. Naturally a man who had to gamble pushed a hard bargain – the bad season was his opportunity. Then he bought up the tiller to whom he had earlier advanced this mysterious form of power – credit. The first financier was driven to be hard. He had a stronger sense of the future than the others, and he had had to capitalise that sense. So his natural wish to bank was aggravated by the danger in which he was put by the resentment of the laggard producers. There was no limit at which he could say his margin of safety might stand. He must store and buy up, drive up interest and make the traffic bear every ounce it could. He had foresight, it was true, but that very foresight revealed to him how precarious were his fortunes and how few might be the seasons in which the stupid sense of the community would, without an outburst of lynching, let him drive his bargains. That is the atmosphere in which business has grown up and that is why business is not social, nor sensible, nor easy – but business. So money is hated as the plague and spread like it, for, as again the proverbs say, money talks. The world was becoming international, and here was the first international medium of communication.

We have seen how inevitable was the rise of

money, how it was only another symptom of man's growing consciousness, of the power of his emerging intelligence to make from the outer world the abstractions which should give him more power and so more vision. We have seen, that as this is so, how it is that the very power which fights the money power, the sense of the individual's rights, springs from the same source as the money power. The first banker, daringly advancing his capital to an inefficient, agriculturally ignorant cultivator and, even more daringly, foreclosing on the farm when the cultivator crashed, and the first prophet, denouncing this 'unnatural' but inevitable advance, are really but two sides of the same problem. The banker is the pioneer individualist trying with the new means of individualism to make good. The prophet is the individualist stating the rights of the laggard individuals. He claims for them, each to have his place, to be unexploited, to carry on in the old inefficient way and yet to have a protection – each with a right to exist in his own right – which the earlier community certainly never guaranteed its constituents. It is perhaps not without significance that one of the first two prophets, Amos – the 'herdsman' of Tekoa – was probably a farmer of some substance whose district had begun to feel the pinch of the Samarian bankers.

II

Whether it was the influence of the prophets or, as seems more likely, the military confusion of the area from which we hear their voices, the money power did not take the next step in its development in the Levant nor indeed on the mainland. It was among the trading islands of the Ægean, one of the poles between which currency first began to flow, that money first had its full social consequences. For it was here that specific monetary form of social power, the Tyranny, appeared and flourished. It is to the work of Mr. P. N. Ure that we owe the detection of this important phase in social evolution. The Tyrant (whose name of course implies not a peculiar violence in the exercise of power but rather a peculiar unprecedentness in the obtaining of it) is really the Hero in business. When the Hero first appears with his intense individuality which renders him free of tabus, immune to tribe suggestibility and aware only of physical power, he requires only good muscles and a sharp sword and courage to win him followers and then loot for himself and his band. When the world on which he preys has itself become individualised he needs more cunning to attain his ends. Money then becomes his main weapon. He trades, pirates, is middle man, conveyer, taxer. He stimulates civilisation's circulation and makes the growing current turn his private mill. But, as such a pioneer must be something of an outcast, he has to make his own strong room and guard it himself. So he buys up the loose men whom the new, brisker circulation of trade is carrying round the world, 'masterless men,' loose cells, torn out of the agricultural matrix of the old settled social groups, and now, with no purpose in life but to exist for themselves, looking for anyone who will keep them. So we see employer and employees united by the same socially-disintegrative process. Such a man is Polycrates, Tyrant of Samos. He is possessed of an island base large enough to be a fortress not to be taken save by forces whose concentrated attention his extinction would not repay. So the Persian Empire endures this carefully ensconced leech on its flank. He battens and grows fabulously in wealth. And no doubt, like most parasites, he was not merely an extractor, but by his trading activities put something back into the loosely articulated civilisation out of which he helped himself so handsomely. Finally he is caught by the neighbouring satrap and his social status shown by the fact that he is impaled. Indeed the Tyrants of their nature are unstable beings. No divinity hedges them. They have no prescriptive right. They have to put all their cards on the table, and when they cannot play them better than anyone else they must go under. There they stand with no shrouds of mystery to hide them; their line of defence little more than a counter. No doubt they have their guards, but each guard has in his knapsack more than the marshal's baton, the crown

itself. They are loyal, not for reverence but because
of their pay, and when it will pay better to revolt
than serve, then they will serve their master as he
served the old order. If authority must always
forget a dying king there is no one it forgets more
quickly than the novus rex whose novelty has failed
to deliver the goods. But trade, money and mercenaries are not the only marks of the Tyrant. The
clue to his character is that he is an individualist.
So he will welcome innovation. He is not afraid
of enterprise; on the contrary, he knows that his
kingdom is a business that depends on forestallment.
He must patronise every originality, for not only
must he keep his own nature supple but he must
break the adhesion of the people he rules and make
them able to see that their life is one which depends
no longer on unquestioned custom demanded by
social conscience, but on innovations which can
show cash returns to the individual to-day. So as
Tyranny develops and spreads on to the mainland
of Greece we can see the tyrants at the social tasks
that illustrate their problems and their characteristic
reaction to them.

Here, then, is the character of the first business
state; the Tyrant constant and fertile in enterprise;
his mercenaries picked from every country that
could yield soldiers of fortune, men whose only
price was good pay and who had only one criterion
for a master that he should be successful; his people
desperately distracted by their factions (for the

heralds of most Tyrannic *coups d'état* were the internecine quarrels of aristocrat, oligarch and democrat) and then again amusedly distracted by his displays. All this is a picture of a society riddled with individualism and unstable to the point of collapse. So the tyrannies fail to make good because it is a pre-sociological political science that dares teach that societies can be held together by no cohesive force save the wish of each individual to have a good and better time and the fear that he may not.

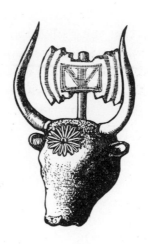

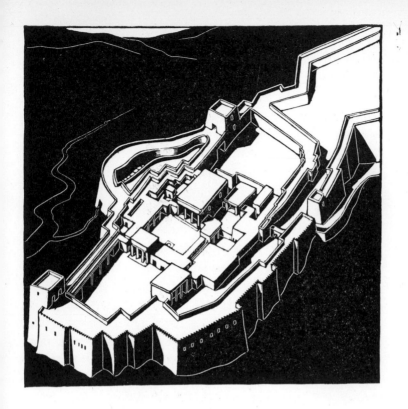

CHAPTER VII

THE FIRST SEA POWER AND THE IRON-BEARING LORDS

I

BUT before we trace the stage beyond Tyranny, man's next stage of emergence, his next attempt to rule himself and, in this particular phase, to make the money power social, let us look round the

civilised world. The sixth century B.C. is now here.
We have man's emergent mind giving him a new
religion, a religion of individual morality, a religion
that tries to recompose the decomposing homogeneous state by making the heterogeneous individuals, it has become, balance out on an elaborate
and alas! abstract concept of rights and duties. The
same phase in the development of his mind also
gives rise to money, banking, usury, and so, by
destroying the primitive cultivator, disintegrates
further the early state. For now, instead of an
immemorial labour that kept before men's eyes their
connection with the land, a labour in which those
who toiled most wearily yet had prescriptive place,
dignity and even right, we have the men of power
at the head becoming contemptuous, moneyed, non-
toiling owners of the land on which their chattels –
serfs to-day, slaves to-morrow – toiled with ever-
growing discouragement. And finally we have,
where commerce is most brisk, the money power
made fully political and given autocracy in the form
of the Tyrant.

It is easy to look upon the outline of this evolution
as one of decline. Is not man becoming increasingly
wretched, the prey of ever more ruthless cunning
and violence? This sketch of history is not directed
to prove that every day and in all respects man has
been getting better and better. The aim of this
essay is to see whether under all the increasing
complexity of history a single process and a single

cause can be discovered. What is the most fundamental unit which throughout history might have given rise to all the changes that have made up history? It seems that to find that basic current we must penetrate below action to character, and that it is the emergence of man's spirit as self-conscious, critical intelligence which is the clue to and explanation of all his acts, both mistakes and achievements. And certainly that process has not failed, nor does it show sign of failure. Painful and tragic it may be, but if the attainment of consciousness and understanding is the aim of life, then not only has man done his part so far but he is continuing to do it with increasing insight and energy. So what we have viewed so far, that part of history during which a new phase of intensified consciousness was changing all his habits, may without undue optimism be called a period when expansion was everything. It is always necessary that man should first win new powers. It comes next that he has to learn how to carry them. Inevitably his first wieldings are ill-co-ordinated, clumsy, dangerous and full of accidents. Much that looks like violence, closer examination shows is really weakness of control. Much that has passed for cunning can be seen to be the involuntary secretiveness of a creature that finds itself, by the same event, cut off and become strange to its former associates and provided by its very separation with almost impregnable defences.

What we see presented to us as we continue to

follow the story of man's emergence is, now, man's reaction to his new powers – after expansion, co-ordination; after a variety of new capacities and inventions, new channels and new aims. Had man's history really been a tragic one, had he proved but the sport of a destiny too vast for him to bear, then this is the period, about this sixth century B.C., when his new powers would have disrupted him and he would have gone back to animalism. The new ferments of his mind would have burst the social systems in which he lived, and through which the building of civilisation is made possible. And either he would have recovered again the animal instincts which make it possible for gregarious beasts to struggle on and reproduce or, perhaps more likely, a failure as a man, he would have proved even more of a disaster as a feral beast and shortly have become extinct. Often we talk lightly of the return of barbarism. Do we ever define what we mean? In the first place there are many barbarisms and many savageries. To which do we intend to lapse? And they are all elaborate ways of life – inevitable to their constituents, in their passing time and their restricted space, but probably quite impossible to anyone else. And in the second place are we certain that if we collapsed from the present arduous but not too arduous front, we could find a comfortable base-line where we could stabilise? It is extremely doubtful. Anthropology has not as yet gone far, but already it has shown that all societies are

equally old and all equally elaborate. The elaboration of an individualised society is different from
that of one ruled by tabus, but the one is not less
complex than the other. It may be that there is no
more chance of our civilisation going back to barbarism than of such a failing side line in evolution,
say as the duck-billed platypus – a creature not
quite a mammal and not quite a reptile – becoming
a lizard. Both lizard, mammal, and platypus are
now equally old, equally committed to their line,
and they cannot be shunted across on to each other's
lines. More must be said about this pre-anthropo-
logical fancy about barbarism when later this essay
deals with the close of the Roman Empire. Here it
is enough to point out that certainly in the sixth
century, after a period of profound unsettlement and
expansion, a period when the moulds of the old
societies were cracked and new raw men and raw
experience poured into the gaps, man gave a most
impressive display of his power of pulling himself
together, of accepting the new and building it up
with the old into a larger and more powerful system.
For this sixth century marks the emergence of
Levantine civilisation from its second dark age, or
as its new members would have thought, the rise
of a new order, a new classicism from a period of
freedom and romance. The first great classic æon,
the period during which human societies were
co-ordinating their functions, developing to the
utmost everything they possessed but admitting no

more raw material into their workshop, that period seems to have terminated, as had earlier periods, with a similar boiling over of the patriarchal plains-men. Whether these invasions were partly caused by new inventions on the part of the plains-men, the horse, for instance (which is first heard of as the Ass of the East in Hammurabi's time) – or whether they were provoked by drought and the failure of the grasslands or by huge increase of population – there can be no doubt that as most murders require not only a murderer but a murderee, so civilisation at these times of deluge is always highly provocative. Certainly it was never more so than before this Deluge, which was to lay the alluvium from which the most creative civilisation man had yet achieved was to spring. The old civilisation was rich and full of new stuffs; it was distracted with internecine wars, and the ties that held the constituents each to his nation were loosened and confused. An united civilisation has never had anything to fear from the simpler, weaker, less persistent and more poorly equipped types that hang about its frontiers. Civilisation, like the female, is in most cases only captured when through inner need she feels the necessity of capture. By the sixth century, Levantine civilisation had already undergone another such fertilising. The Minoan civilisation, the first thalassocracy, based upon Crete, had been swept away and its memory so lost that save in the tale of Theseus no rumour of the island empire's greatness remained.

Yet it had been a very distinctive step in civilisation. Here was a mixed population made of two strains, a northern and a southern, possessed of a base large enough to make them powerful and sufficiently detached to make them secure. Their kings were therefore forerunners of the Tyrants, such as Polycrates on his smaller Samos. Their future was on the sea, first no doubt as raiders and then, increasingly, as traders. North lay coasts to which came much of the strange wealth of the dim trackless lands that stretched without end. South lay Egypt offering a market for their raw stuffs and ready to send back goods. How early and how wide was that traffic archæological chemistry has traced like a detective. In the dusty corner of an early Pharaoh's tomb, rifled æons ago, careful search found the broken ferule of one of his staffs. It was of gold and so was unperished. But, more, it was of a peculiar gold – gold, showed the analysis, in which there was also the metal antimony. Now there is but one mine in the ancient world where gold combined with antimony is found. It is up in the Danube basin. So it seems, so early was traffic between the north and the south being carried.

The sea traders grew rich. Their's was an intense life. They lived obviously at high pressure. They crowded their whole town under one roof, living more densely than any human society before or since, so that their close, intricate dwelling became for ever the symbol of elaborate structure, and what

they called Labry-Rinthos – the Double Axe's City –
became for all time The Labyrinth. In this close
city they crowded even more closely at the heart to
watch the frantic violence of the hugh bulls stam-
peding in the pit ring and the frantic agility of their
slave toreadors who, in the restricted space, must
elude the beast's plunge by leap-frogging over its
sweeping horns. And not content with this intensely
congested life, it may be as a natural reaction to it,
these strange people braced and wound themselves
until it would seem physical construction could go
no further and the heart must have been crushed so
that they could not draw breath. But as the hand
of the boxer is wound in the cestus, as the wrist of
the wrestler is gripped by the bandlet, so the figures
of these strange creatures were bound. Their cities
hung like wasp nests on the hillsides, whence like
wasps they swarmed out to sweep the seas. The
inhabitants were not only wasp-tempered and wasp-
nested but actually wasp-waisted too. We have seen
what an important part tattoo and cosmetic must
have played in making man distinguish himself. We
have seen how later in Egypt the secondary sexual
characteristic of hair was first removed and then in
symbolic form for social purposes replaced. Here too
in Crete we see again a culture which had a curious
connection with an habiliment which was both an
appearance and a sensation.[1] Whatever the source

---

[1] The whole of this subject: the connection between dress and
larger action, needs writing out. First undoubtedly comes the wish

of its power or however it managed to exploit it, Crete came upon a period of exhaustion. She had spread her strange metallic culture on to the mainland, and in Tyrens and Mycenæ dwelt strange-shaped, cunning, wealthy rulers like those who dwelt in the mother hives up in the rocks of Crete. The glitter of one of those rare human insects may be found in the pages of Homer, for there can be little doubt that the picture of King Alcinoos in his brazen house is made up from real fragments. Here on the rough page we find clinging a gleaming

for distinctiveness and distinction: the interest of discerning where the actual frontier of primary sensation lies, beyond which there is the vast world of secondary sensation. These two worlds must first have been confused, and to distinguish them must have been a decisive human step. Then comes the discovery that this frontier is not really distinct and can be modified. First hair can be cut and then plucked, nails can be cut, teeth can be filed and pierced. Appearance can be completely changed and sensations can be modified. Then ear lobes, septa and lips can be pierced, circumcisions and incisions can be made more and more extensive and daring. The waist can be restricted to a quarter of its natural size, the foot can be equally sub-formed and even the shape of the skull, the most resistant part of the skeleton and, one would have thought, the most dangerous to modify, can be pressed completely out of its norm. And all these modifications have a double aspect: there is first the deliberate change of appearance, the sense that man, though in an animal body, can disguise his animalism (the reason often given for filing and blacking teeth is that dogs have sharp white teeth), and there is, also equally important, the sensation, the direct feeling, of being different. Complete health is complete unconsciousness of the body. So we may understand why some sensualists purposely, though unconsciously, become hyperchondriacs. To be completely constricted is to become completely physically-individually self-conscious. So men and women like to be braced and bound and strung not merely for the appearance but for the feeling of restraint that, acting as a stimulant, renders them more alive and active (see Behaviourism, where all our future activities are attributed to our first restrictions). It may be that, physiologically, great constriction, such as tight-lacing, may compress indirectly the solar plexus, cause glandular congestion, and drive blood to the brain.

scale or two of the extinct species. The man who sang the magic of the metal palace sang the rude but more living power that swept away its elaborate material achievement.

II

Yet the 'Iron-bearing lords,' that made the doom of Crete final, were for long, far too alive to do more than live. Men so lusty need no restrictions. Their wills need no canalising to store them up and husband the gentle current so that it may reach its goal. Their force was direct and their goals were close. Restriction to poor land and poverty of technique made the simplest achievements wonderful. To have enough meat, enough spoil, enough slaves, enough women – could mind foresee will and appetite ever reaching such goals? To forge a sword that would not turn its edge or shatter, and harness as splendid as fancy – all life might be taken up in such craft. The perfect technique of the Minoans was gone. The absolute naturalism which they had attained and which to them may well have seemed futile, a dead wall, was now, by the loss of technique, safely out of reach of their conquerors. These might gape and scrawl, long for such gifts and attempt with all their power to imitate. They could not know that the men who had such powers had suddenly by their exercise arrived at a paralysing weakness. The eye and hand which could copy all

it saw, free of any help of order or convention,
was prying near the end of desire and the brink of
the Bathos. Perhaps only the creator dare see his
creation apart from any purpose to which it may
be put or any frame of reference into which it may
be fitted. Certain it appears that with technical
mastery there must come a moment when pattern,
and with it purpose, vanish. Man glimpses the
whole, infinite, astounding incoherence. It is not
that he sees nothing as an end, but rather everything. There are no means. Everything is in its
own right and an end. Though all is connected,
every unit is equally connected with all. So nothing
leads to any one thing more than to any other. All
the doors, as in Ali Baba's tale, are all marked and
doors are on every side. Design, achievement,
causation vanish in the infinitely variegated surface
of the continuum. Man sees that purpose, aim and
striving were only fancy patterns he projected on the
outer world. He now sees it as it is. He must either
be content, acceptingly, unstrivingly to contemplate
it, or he must fall back to the animal level where
starved appetite is still channelled and confined and
conserved by rigid circumstance.

So we see how it is that a classic period exhausts
itself. It cannot sustain itself on naturalism because
naturalism means for it complete incoherence – the
contradiction of art. Nor can it go on with convention, for it was because it had so mastered and surmounted all convention that it emerged inevitably

on to this bleak platform of masterly but ineffective naturalism. No convention can be deliberately readopted.[1] Indeed to talk so is a contradiction in words. It is but as a by-product that the exercise of a convention gives inner satisfaction. It is not so intended. Its purpose is to be an instrument whereby man may grasp and draw to himself so much of the reality outside him. If naturalism has failed then let man realise what has befallen him. The choice is not his to go back and cousin himself that he is again a child. The only choices are these: Either to realise that his life is over; to see in the failure of naturalism, the writing on the wall, the reading on the chart, the mark on the clinical thermometer, which shows that his time is up, his power over, his fate sealed; or to realise that he must go forward regardless of rendering or sense, press on against reality however incoherent it may seem to be becoming, and determine to die, if die he must, still exploring and not in retreat. This crisis it would seem has repeatedly faced man and though, naturally on the first occasion he did not put his doubts and struggles into writing, he had to face them, and his conduct, and, so, much of history, is explained by them.

[1] A dying classic period will, because it is completely individualised, take to eclecticism and this, because invention is exhausted, will have to throw back to earlier styles to get itself variety. Hence archaic types are copied and we get archaisticism at the close of ages of art. But though it borrows the form of a convention it does so in order to express an anti-conventional spirit.

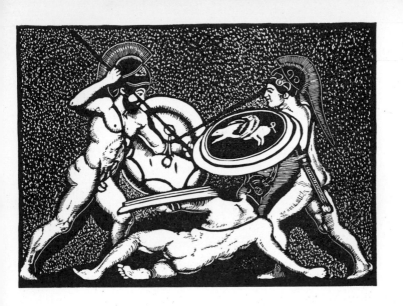

CHAPTER VIII

THE LAW-GIVERS, POLITICAL AND NATURAL

I

EVERY age of complete achievement must therefore tend to become one of complete exhaustion, and civilisations may be said to collapse through a double process, the completeness of the outlook of the man of that day and the finitude – the inadequate finitude – of their sense of pattern. It is not unnatural, therefore, that as after the *fin de siècle* should come the Deluge, after the Deluge should, as inevitably, come the re-emergence. The age of the

167

Iron-Bearing Lords, who had smashed the Minoan culture, and of whom Hesiod wearily sings, the age that had shut Egypt within its bounds, the age which brought down as far as the Judean hills the darkness of the obliterating Cimmerians, through which we hear the voice of the Lamentations, this age was rapidly to be succeeded, it was to give rise to an age of unprecedented law-giving and ordering. Indeed, the law-givers are its peculiar characteristic and contribution to civilisation. The Tyrants, whether like Polycrates, recapitulating on a petty scale the sea-merchant principality of Crete, or whether like Peisistratus, a good type of the later Tyrant, foreshadowing the banker despots of the Italian Renaissance, these men are only an aspect of this period of Emergence.

Nor are the prophets the real characters of the age. They are a variant but not a dominant. They failed in the main. The type which is of chief significance is the Law-giver; and not only for what he stands himself, but for the type to which he gave rise, the philosopher. Law-giving had, of course, been done before. Hammurabi the Great, who combined Sumer and Akad about 2000 B.C. and eventually found it necessary if his amalgam was to bind that it should be given a code, promulgated decrees. But they were probably rules which circumstances had already outlined, and the part of his law which is most important is therefore probably not the regulations themselves but their sanction. That, the

King had to say, was not his own authority, which any rationalist would have thought more than adequate, for he was a most successful conqueror, but the authority of the King's God, the Sun. We see then that the code of Hammurabi shows Sun worship, a worship that probably started in the desert, made suitable to an elaborate agricultural and urban society. We know, too, that after the collapse of Aknaton's 'heresy' the energetic general, Horemheb, who took the throne promulgated a Law which may have been an adaptation and modernisation of the current customs in so far as the 'new religion' had disturbed men's minds and made an influential few demand a restatement.

Moses also, however much his Law must have been elaborated by later editors, must have adapted, for the wandering tribes he led, a code out of the Egyptian morality. But with the dawn of 'the Greek Renaissance' the Law-giver appears neither as King nor Magician but *sui generis*. The age of iron and action was over, the age of reflection and reason must take its place. The invaders had smashed the old society and even before they smashed it, we have seen, it is more than probable that the spirit had already left it. There had remained on, the form, the form of a magic-sanctioned society, or, as the present writer would prefer to put it, a society of such ancient and unquestioned authority and so, of such suggestive force that no one thought of disobeying or altering its elaborate tissue of rules. This ancient form of society, as elaborate as the organism of our body, had been a single living organism, and the elaborateness of the one was no more questioned than the ordinary man questions the elaborateness of the other – as long as it lived. Gradually, however, the single informing will had contracted, been distributed among and condensed into each of the constituents, and so, when struck from without, the social elaborations, instead of being the channels through which a single will might strike back, only rendered ineffective such resistance as the individualised constituents might have put up. Because, therefore, the invaders had smashed the elder societies, and these had already been disintegrated by individualism, the invaders for long built up nothing. Even their way of living showed the disparateness of their characters from the character of the people whom they had overthrown. We have seen the Minoans, for example, lived in settlements that necessitated literally a shoulder to shoulder existence. The conquerors from the North lived, as we shall see in their turn the Norse raiders lived, out at large upon the land. Such was the looseness of their social structure, so much were they simply families that coalesced for fighting and not citizens, that they liked to live, as the back-veldt Boer boasts to-day he wishes to live, out of sight of even the smoke of his neighbour. But at length settled life necessitated settlements. Men tired of fighting and there was less and less to fight for. Spoil was spent, hunting could not sustain the increasing population. Agriculture must be pursued with all the energy that men had given to the fight and the chase. The crafty and capable Ulysses, though he might trade and could fight, could also handle well the plough. A settled life necessitated that the settlers also come to some agreement with the disorganised, but not exterminated natives.

To drift in eddies was to see even themselves, the lords, go down into chaos. As long as they were flooding down on to fresh lands they kept their ranks and, like a tide of billows, swept on. But when the invasions reached the land's limits then, like waves against rock, they broke back in cross-currents and confusion upon each other. The individualism which had made them follow Heroes for adventure had no outlet. Now they were settled there was no Hero leadership to draw forth the only loyalty which such individuals could feel. As example of the two ways in which these difficulties were solved at this time we can take the two classic examples of law-giving among the people most individualised, the Greeks.

II

In the extreme south of the land a small settlement of Northern raiders were trying to preserve themselves from disintegration. They had done little more than make a landing. The natives had been pushed up into the hills. They could not resist openly, but the country offered great opportunities for guerilla tactics. What should the Spartans do? They might either deliberately expand or deliberately contract. A policy and plan they must have. Under the direction of Lycurgus they decided to attempt to stabilise action; to preserve themselves for ever as a fighting organisation. This proved in the end a mistake. The Spartans were at heart cowards. They were afraid of the future, afraid of the magic of their surroundings and neighbours, afraid of what they did not understand in themselves. They put themselves on the defensive because they determined to be exclusive. They set time against them because they resolved that their hard and narrow constitution should be immutable. The consequences might have been expected. The one aim of the Lycurgan constitution was to make a permanent invincible war-machine. That is always a sign of fear and weakness, because permanent war cannot be the aim of any creature. The wild beast can fight, but it will generally avoid doing so if there is any way out. The raiding pirate will spoil as long as there are rich and weak places to be raided. But war for war's sake is the proposal of an unbalanced mind. As little as the civilised can, the wild approve such an inverted morality. So Lycurgus failed in all his objectives. The military machine grew out of date and was smashed by the Theban phalanx as invented by Epaminondas. Even the Peloponnese was never united; while within their own bounds, such was the state of fear in which the Spartans lived, that they were always having recourse to the ghastly practice of the Crypteia. These men, who looked upon themselves as the noblest of soldiers, felt that they had to practise against their wretched slaves a form of secret assassination which makes even hounded revolutionaries contemptible. These men, who cultivated bravery as their religion, could bring themselves to creep by night upon the miserable homesteads of their serfs, set light to the dwelling and stab the creatures who broke from the flames. Beside this evidence of group paranoia, their incurable thievishness and the fact that when abroad a Spartan could seldom resist selling his country for gold, are almost amiable failings. The state, too, was incapable of keeping its form. Gradually the double kingship – a curious survival and weakness which Lycurgus might well have used his power to abolish – became purely a generalship, and the power passed into the hands of the administrators – the Ephors. Altogether the Spartan constitution and state combine to give perhaps the most interesting record we have from this stage of man's emergence of the effort which he made to arrest his growth, and the vain and morbid consequences of such an effort. For when we consider all its features and symptoms there can be no doubt that we are presented with a deliberate attempt at atavism. Lycurgus recognised that individualism had come, he realised also that

the old heroic raiding phase was over. Should the
Dorians grow up and blend, giving their energy to
the common stock of a Greek culture and taking
from the earlier inhabitants their tradition of art
and technical skill, their delicacy of hand and mind?
Lycurgus decided to kill the possibility of growth.
The Spartans, like the Tartar and the Turk in their
turn, should remain camped in a land he exploited.
The choice was fatal. Sparta perished because of her
mistake. Lycurgus could not veto growth any more
than Canute could veto the tide. But the tragedy
of Sparta was not only its own. Its activity and its
example did much to ruin all Greece. The spirit of
exclusiveness rendered that culture fatally weak and
finally gave it to its conquerors.

Such was one of the attempts of the Law-giver to
deal with the new situation: the newly settled
individuals – it was to crush them back into the
mould of an iron constitution and to re-create a
State which, with the individual reassimilated,
should be eternal. But constitutions cannot undo
the psyche. The other attempt was far wiser and
more fruitful. It is the constitution connected with
the name of Solon and its fruit was the culture that
was most Greek, the art and enterprise of Athens.
Solon seems to have realised that the problem before
him was to make a living people preserve their
continuity; while to Lycurgus the problem seems to
have presented itself in the falsely simplified form,
how best to preserve unmodified, arrested, the Sparta

he knew. Solon, it seems, after a preliminary failure, prepared himself for his task by spending some years of enforced absence in Egypt. A man who with the mind of a Greek lived in Egypt could not have fallen into the mistake of thinking that states are kept together by military force. Coming from Egypt he must have carried with him a clear knowledge of the importance of the imponderables. Yet Egypt, with its elaborate state religion, was even in the Saite Dynasty a going concern: an organism that had its own momentum and rhythm. It could not be transplanted to highly individualised Athens. The constitution must therefore give the fullest opportunities of growth consonant with the preservation of the community. Solon's task was immense. For in the first place he found the poorer sort sunk in such debt that he was compelled to enact the abolition of their indebtedness. Such a step was of course what Repudiation is in our day. It meant that the state to avoid a social split had to face an economic writing down of capital which, though it might stave off revolution, would sweep away from the strong and capable much of the basis of their attachment to society. Solon was up against money, and like most Dictators he thought more of social solidarity than of economic soundness. No doubt his choice of evils was the right one, but ignorance of economics had to be paid for later. For money flouted, not understood, again accumulated in the hands of the capable, and from this sprang that late form of Tyranny, that of Peisistratus. Solon's Remission had not cured the evil. The poor again were unable to meet their obligations, and this time it was not a Law-giver but a paymaster who paid off their debts and made himself by such business ability master of the people. It was because the ancient world didn't understand money and would try and think in terms of that stubborn conservatism which it called justice that it had every now and then to be foreclosed upon by the Banker type. Like the Medici, Peisistratus not only adorns Athens with great buildings to illustrate his power and make all men realise his resources as well as his care for the common good and his acceptability to the gods: he not only has the text of Homer set down in writing (till then carried in mind by the Rhetoricians who recited the divine saga): such a setting down of tradition is always sign of crystallisation in a people's history: but he also attends, very significantly, to the actual worship of his subjects. He causes popular cults to be changed when these cults would remind the people of a version of the past he does not wish them to remember. Athens might hear of Homer's Greece. Was not Peisistratus himself a modern Hero, and anyhow Athens, because it had played so little part in the Homeric struggle, could not draw from the canon any special political lesson, other than that it became her to be Greek. But more local cults must be remodelled to serve the group or at least not to distract from loyalty to the reigning house.

Nevertheless, in spite of all his enterprise and in spite of the fact that he did represent a side of the social problem, the economic side, which Solon had handled with insufficient care, Peisistratus and his house are only an episode, for psychological factors are more important than economic factors, and it was these latter that the Law-giver was attempting to solve while the Tyrant made the miscalculation of thinking that men would stay quiet if only you paid them not to make trouble.

So we can say that with all his mistakes it is the Law-giver who is typical and significant of this age, and there can be little doubt that these two classic Law-givers illustrate the two ways in which the mind of men when it becomes individualised reacts to the social problem with which it finds itself faced. One is the way of Democracy and the other the way of Militarism. Both are advances out of a simpler, less intentional frame of mind. But one leads to growth and the other to cataclysm. Yet even to-day civilisation has not definitely made up its mind to which it will commit itself.

III

So we see the small states of Greece through their Law-givers precipitating their constitutions. The States are now manned with individuals – the old homogeneous mass is disintegrated. An architect must be found to build them all together so that as

M

wall and arch made from thousands of separate stones stand as units and interlock as one house, so men and classes may become one state. But even in Athens we must note the individualism almost defeated the invention designed to co-ordinate it. The state was never stable and, even when it endured, its dimensions were only what the modern world would have called a county. Outside that, the sense of solidarity, always precarious, became quite impossible. Beyond that, Athens could only treat her expanding territories as footstools, and they retaliated by considering her, the free creative democracy, much as a Pole used to consider a Russian.

But the line of man's social evolution does not run down through the collapse of the City-States. Rather it runs tangential to that curve. Man, it is true, is continually throwing off new types of society, but these societies are only symptoms of his mental evolution and projections of his emergent mind. They express that mind so long as they are growing, for they are responding to its needs and are its outward and visible signs. But as soon as they decline, they are at best its prison. We do not learn about life by studying the withering and collapse of forms from which life has fled. We do not learn about man's emergence by studying the decline and fall of societies of which his creative Spirit has tired. It is not there: it is risen: why seek the living with the dead? Modern history, as was said at the

beginning of this essay, must be concerned with
Man's spirit and only with outward forms as long
as his spirit is building them up to express itself. To
follow the path of that emergent spirit we must
therefore leave the Law-givers and cease to concentrate on such large units (dwarfs though they
politically be) as the city-states themselves. The
Law-giver, as we have seen, is really significant
because he is the type of mind that must next emerge
after the Hero. As the Hero is thrown up to lead a
group which has become so individualised, enterprising and discontented with stable tradition that
its one wish is to swarm, so the Law-giver arises
when that stage is over and the people wish again
to alight.[1] He has the supremely difficult task of
making a good landing. No wonder if he brings it
off and manages to settle the people down, they look
to him with reverence. But in fact he is as transitional a type as the Hero himself. To do his job he
has to be more self-conscious, more reflective a type,
in fact, a higher, more fully emerged man than the
Hero, for the Hero had only to lead them out, while
the Law-giver has to fit and settle them in. But he,
too, is a man of his age, and his age passes quickly
for it is a transitional one. Once the new type of
men, the men but a generation or two descended
from pioneers and soldiers of fortune, newly in-

[1] As we have seen, the Hero phase may be prolonged into the stage
of settlement, by the Hero becoming the Tyrant, but he, too, cannot
last long and social evolution calls out the Law-giver to succeed either
phase of despotism.

dividualised men, once these had settled down, they were not content simply to be observing the laws, holding the frontiers, resisting those who would break in and prosecuting those who would break up. Such a childish sense of ritual might satisfy the Spartans, but not any freer people. Hence, as the Hero is succeeded by the Law-giver, the Law-giver is succeeded by the Philosopher. Men have been forced to think about society, and that has led them to consider the world. So this great age of the sixth century B.C., which has been justly called the dawn of the Greek Renaissance, saw the rise of that distinctive modern type, the Natural Philosopher. The birth of Thales is the birth of a new order of man who will give rise to a new order of society. It is true he is quite a rudimentary type. He depends still mainly upon the empirical methods that slow trial and error had gradually built up through the millennial experience of Egypt. He may have studied in Egypt. If so, he would of course have heard of Psamtek's experiments and, probably, as Greeks were welcome, have had much traditional knowledge brought to his notice. But he opens a new age in understanding because he seems to have conceived the idea of framing from many observations the rudiment of Natural Laws.

He can speculate and can generalise. His speculations also prove practical because he is recorded to have speculated from his meteorological knowledge on the olive crop, to have forestalled on the market and to have made money. Philosophy, when it talks sense in such a simple tongue, can get the ear of the most ordinary.

But original and fertile as his mind undoubtedly was, Thales could never have made explorations in abstract thought, had his setting not been favourable. Society had to be assuring him, if no more, a steady platform from which to take his observations. So his home is really as interesting as himself. We find that he is one of the first – many others, no doubt, are lost – of the philosophers springing up on the fringed western coast of Asia Minor. He came from Miletus; but there were then many small keen towns scattered up and down this coast. As we have seen, it was a frontier of exchange, for on to it came the varied traffic of the islands and down to it came the wealth of the inland kingdoms. The Ægean archipelago was swarming with an adventurous life, too inventive to be called purely practical, but far too set on gain to be quiet enough for speculation. The mainland had already accumulated such wealth as to have become legendary. Gyges and Crœsus were men who could pay much gold for the curious fancied stuffs that came overseas. The seaboard cities trafficked much and saw much of two worlds. They were balanced between the too active life of the free sailors of the small islands and the too passive life of the subjects of the rich wide-territoried despots of the inland. And, as the first life probably appeared in the warm sheltered pools between the

too restless sea and the too immobile land, so here
on the Ionian coast appeared the new life of the
speculative and creative mind.

There it grows for a few generations until the
next change in human history compels it to move.
But by that time it is ready to be transplanted and
the seed of a new understanding takes root in the
islands, travels over the mainland of Greece, goes to
Magna Græcia (which is yet to become Italy),
spreads also to Egypt, until the whole of the Eastern
Mediterranean is alive with the new knowledge and
philosophy has raised itself a monument which no
deluge of barbarism has been able to overwhelm.

But before following this, the central development of mind, we must see how the slower development of more backward minds was to push philosophy into the sea and on to the islands. We have
seen that in the seventh century B.C., a sudden
condensation took place in the minds of men. They
turned from the traditional Fertility, or Life Religion, to one of individual observance. The old erotic
rites were suppressed. Now the result of this change
and this repression was twofold. Either they might
make the individual concentrate with all his new
isolated energy on the salvation of his soul after
death, and so they were to lead to the collapse of
the societies in which such individuals predominated,
or the consequence might prove to be clean contrary. The new individuals, no longer assuaged by
ancient rites, would turn their energy to conquest,

especially to the conquest of what they considered now to be the old depraved religions out of which they had come into their new and moral gospel. They would become the first crusaders. In that area and section – the Levantine section of civilisation – (which in this essay we are taking as the example from which to illustrate the whole process of civilisation at this stage) – probably these two types – though individuals may overlap – are not contemporaneous but successive. The first reaction of the type of mind that comes with the new Puritan religion, is to crusade and to hew in pieces the decadent, depraved idolators. The next reaction is to concentrate on one's own soul's salvation and to desert the world and take up asceticism, with the future life completely eclipsing the present. Certain it is that the rise of the Persian Empire – the first of the great Empires – begins to reveal itself increasingly under research as something like a crusade and similar to that other great outburst of military conquest from the wide spaces, the Arab invasions that immediately succeeded their acceptance of Mohammedanism. Professor Herzfeld seems to have proved that Zoroaster, under whose teaching religion in Persia goes through the revolution from a traditional, impersonal, a-Moral Religion of Life to a personal religion of morality, abstinence and salvation, was actually protected and championed by Hystaspes. He it was whose son became Darius, and some see behind his irresistible military forces the greater force of an idea for which the minds of men were ripe. The Persian Empire, it seems, owed its immense success to the same power that afterwards gave an even greater empire to the Caliphs. It was the same power that also gave the genius of Napoleon the first opportunity to outbreak: for his Italian campaign in which his military gifts were first recognised, owed its success quite as much to the Revolutionary enthusiasm of his soldiers and the welcome these ideas had already found in Italy, as to his strategy.

This movement changed the face of the ancient world. We can see, all as part of a consistent, if not conscious policy, that Cyrus puts back the Jews in their country there to continue a religious evolution with which the Persian genius was so much in sympathy: that Cambyses, violent and perhaps epileptic, showing instead of tolerance the reverse, is really advancing the same puritan revolution when he despoils the temple and tombs of Egypt.

Evidently, too, even this violence does not awake active resentment, but perhaps even a secret sympathy; because we know that it is at this date that the new religious spirit shows itself, springing distinctively from Egyptian soil. For this is the date when the Hermetic writings appear in Egypt, writings which, for the first time in Egypt, set forth the puritan ideas of an abstinent, individual life here, rewarded by an eternal individual life after death. And these earliest of writings can be dated because they mention with respect the Persian satrapy.[1]

The force which spread over the whole of the Levant pushed on with the unifying irresistibility with which, later, Mohammedanism was to advance over much of the same area. The Lydian kingdom went down before it, and, reaching the coast, the Ionian cities also were swept under. Philosophy took then, to the sea, for though the force behind the Persian advance was at bottom the same force that was making men speculate, the earlier form of simple conviction and action was incompatible with its later form, speculation. Persia offered greater freedom, a higher standard of individuality, than the ancient world had known. There was religious toleration. The later persecution of all other religions by the Magi, under the Parthian and Sassanian Dynasties, seems to have been a decadence. Cambyses' violence was an exceptional outburst. The spirit of the early Persian Empire is that of Cyrus' Proclamation, and the state religion was a religion of individuality. But the Greeks, in their cities, had enjoyed such intensive growth that they had gone beyond that. Probably the Persian standard of spiritual life and intellectual freedom was as high as any society dare go and not be politically unstable. But what cared the Greeks for such a humdrum

[1] See *The Doctrine of the Future Life in Egypt prior to the rise of Christianity*, by Flinders Petrie. The author definitely states that prior to these writings there is no reference in Egyptian literature to a life of abstinence and abandonment being pleasing to the Gods.

thing as political stability! They were only concerned to follow speculation wherever it might lead, wholly ignorant of the fact that this new sense was a faculty untried before in the world and capable, maybe, of producing disastrous consequences; perhaps, even, the dissolution of society and so the destruction of this very civilisation which they were rearing.

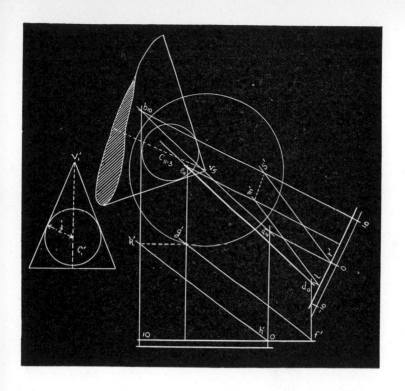

CHAPTER IX

THE PROMISE AND FAILURE OF
THE SCIENTIFIC STATE

I

SUCH is the distribution of civilisation at the end of
the sixth century. The emergence of humanity has
reached a stage when we have to recognise a very
interesting and very perilous condition. The ad-

187

vance has been so rapid that a new danger begins to appear. The main danger for the first men had been from other animals. The main danger for the first civilised men has been from savages. The main danger for the highly civilised men of the sixth century was a double one: they were endangered by the very length of civilisation: the small intense societies of Greece were in danger from the vast expansive society of Persia. Both States were distinctive productions of civilisation; but neither could accept the other. It is equally true to point out that the secessionalism of the Greeks would not accept a place in the Persian Empire (which could grant the tolerance which permitted Judaism to continue its religious and moral evolution) as it is to say that Persia would not tolerate Greece. The other side of this danger was not only the length of civilisation, that there were now a series of waves all following one another and that as the impulse of the leading wave gave out or was checked, the waves coming on behind would overtake it, overwhelm it and bring the whole advance to confusion. It was that the front wave could not escape this fate of being overtaken, because itself it was bound to break up into a confusion of cross-waves. The highest civilisation is bound to be the most various, for evolution is always from the simple to the elaborate. In the first advances of civilisation there can be little doubt that those communities which advance, have, on the whole, a better chance of surviving; they were more strong and efficient than those communities which remained conservative and refused to rationalise themselves. But the very process which makes one society go ahead and leave behind the rest, because it is a process of rationalisation, of deliberate modification, foresight, planning, must lead from an enterprising, critical, self-conscious community to an enterprising, critical, self-conscious individual. The pioneer community broke up the primal human stability and became a pirate, and to some extent, a parasite, on the main stock. The pioneer individual, in his turn, will and must play the same trick on the pioneer community that produced him for its own pirate uses. 'Think for yourselves' may be necessary advice to stir men to kick off custom and cast away the sub-rational ties that keep them from pushing violence to extremes. But once they have taken that advice they will not stop content with their community exploiting all the others. They will exploit the community.

There will, therefore, be, at this date, no single unbroken front of civilisation, but a number of divergent and perhaps conflicting raids into the unknown. These varieties will not only be in danger of being swamped from the oncoming mass behind, but they will be in constant conflict with each other. Each unit will be threatened by disruption by its divergent constituents; and the constituents them-selves, self-conscious, frightened, the victims of intense interior conflict, will themselves be in danger of bankruptcy of will and purpose.

Such is the psychological condition of that outbreak of civilisation which began in the sixth century B.C. and which has been named after its finest flower, the Greek Renaissance.

The Greeks are intensely alive, so alive that they are insufficiently concerned with survival. To push on is everything. Regardless of the peril to their base, regardless of exposed flanks, they will penetrate ever further. Accident helps them. The Mediterranean basin was comparatively empty and such inhabitants as it had were easily subdued by men such as the Greek colonists then were, of greater energy and better armed. When the first great organised power, the Empire of Persia, began to spread, it spread from a base so distant from the Greek lands that only the Ionian fringe of their settlements was touched. Persia was at the limit of its expansion where it touched Greece. So, quite apart from their actual resistance, the Greeks were saved by their position. Not for two hundred years was a large expanding state to be their neighbour. Persia, therefore, had enough to do just to hold the tired countries it had seized, quite apart from trying to grasp new, active, distant lands. Persia's own puritan push was declining. She kept going so long because the peoples she ruled were even further declined. Judea, we know, had begun to dream apocalyptically. The best men no longer looked for a good state to be won by their efforts, but awaited the whole order of the world to be instantaneously transformed by Divine intervention. Egypt, we have seen, also was dreaming of another life. The best men there were devoting themselves by renouncing the world to saving their souls after death. And this same movement of personal survivalism was appearing not only among advanced religions such as Egypt's and Judea's, but in the wild highlands of Phrygia. The worship in that place of the Great Mother, there called Cybele, had about this time rapidly developed from an ordinary variant of the general Fertility Religion, into a rite for personal survival after death. Such was the influence of this movement that the black-robed priests of the rite, who were called fanatici, gave their name to all extravagant religious ascetics.

Greece was not yet thinking of personal survival. The people still had enough to do in this life and were too interested in it to be much concerned about a life to come. That concern would come with political failure and scientific discouragement. For the time being they were content to push to its logical conclusions their new individual self-consciousness: (1) by political development, by inventing Democracy – the Right of every individual to be the State's end – and (2) by scientific speculation, by examining the whole of their experience of the outer world in this new, detailed, super-interested way.

Obviously such a world could not last. If Persia

was at its limit both of territorial expansion and the will to spread its culture, then another force must rise and make another empire. For empire building could not cease. The Greeks, it is true, were developing one side of man's mind, his power of understanding the outside world. But their expansion was utterly lop-sided. Their democratic development was not so much an advance in political invention as a deliberate loosening of political structure and a decomposition of the State so as to leave the individual free to expand and speculate regardless of consequences. That this is so is proved by the fact that the Greeks showed not the slightest attempt to federalise their city-states into an effective union. The Amphyctionic Council existed and could have been employed for the purpose; but it was never enabled to take the first step. Indeed, the whole movement was for the city-states themselves to disintegrate further. They would unite to pull down a possible dominant, such as Athens or Sparta, but once that was done they settled back into their real interest, to disintegrate themselves still further, from city-states into party factions *ad infinitum*.

The Persians were at the end of their expansion and had nothing more to say. 'To ride the horse, to shoot straight with the bow and to speak the truth,' to worship the single god of Light whose symbol was the purifying fire and whose service a simple and forceful righteousness, that once had seemed a clean, cleaving gospel, straight as an arrow, strong as a spear, among all the fussy, frowsy tabus and irrational observances. But now it meant less and less. So we shall see all slogans: 'God is One,' 'Men are one and equal,' 'All power to the workers,' must all give out after having seemed in their hour irresistible. For they are not, as their proclaimers believe, revelations; they are only repartees. Men have reached a point when they want an answer to problems to which the old traditional response seems absurdly inapposite. They cannot realise that the problem has arisen because they, themselves, have moved, have changed. The new answer will work well enough to silence the old response. But once that is silenced the new answer will begin to seem equally pointless. For it does not reply to outer experience. It is only a movement away from all group-imposed limitations. It is not a movement towards grasping, embracing, comprehending and unifying all that the new knowledge has brought in of the outer world, and the building it up into an appropriate and satisfying inter-reactive experience.

So the expansion of man, his power not only of taking in more and more of the world, but of using that knowledge to build himself a wider and stronger platform from which to observe it, and a more fully equipped workshop in which to work upon, work up and integrate his raw observation, this essential side of his advance must be taken on by a social organism less lop-sidedly hypertrophied than the Greek and even more simple than the Persian.

II

The society that satisfied this demand lay near the Greek frontier. The Persian base was too distant from Greece to have held those turbulent cities. And also the Persian mind was too advanced; it had followed its own special development too far for the Greek mind to cross-breed with it.

But not only did Macedonia, centred on the town of Pella, lie at the Greek door. These simple highlanders were of Greek ancestral stock. Through the valleys they inhabited had come down the Dorians, the last and not least prized layer in the Hellenic structure. The Macedonians were Greeks who had waited behind, both geographically and psychologically. They held on up in the north under their kings, preserving the primitive strength of their state, while their cousins went geographically south and socially democratic.

So when the time came for the sun of enterprise to thaw this last mass and send it crashing down into the southern valleys they did not come either as blind barbarians or as scornful aristocrats. After a couple of centuries during which the Greeks had continually failed to solve their political problem, but had only made it worse by continual increase of intellectual speculation, here lay the only possible solution.

Philip, their royal genius, the ruler who focused in himself his people's will to advance, is not only a consummate general but, as a statesman, not less able. He has the best war machine of his time and he has used all the inventiveness of genius to make it irresistible. He has learnt how Epaminondas realised that the old traditional Greek line of battle might be improved: how he had changed it from a thin front of spears into such a wedge that the whole mass became one spear, the whole attack could be focused at one point on the enemy's thin uniform front, and that that front so struck, was bound to be pierced, disrupted and scattered. The Macedonian phalanx was a development and improvement of the Theban.

But Philip had no intention of winning with it fruitless victories. To such a genius his army was only the sanction with which to make a people he wished to combine realise the force of his argument. He was no raider, nor was he out after spoils that could be carried off. Indeed, more than a Hero is he the newer type, the Tyrant. For he has in his country a weapon even more to his hand than his highland soldierly and the tactics of his new phalanx. He had some of the chief gold mines of the ancient world. He struck from these a coinage which did as much for the spread of money power as had the Lydian invention done three centuries before. For Philip's gold staters travelled all over the ancient world until, within a couple of centuries, rude smiths, as far away as England,[1] are striking curious

[1] Sir John Evans, *Coins of Ancient Britons*, p. 21

stylisations which are degenerate recollections of the quadriga that adorned the coinage of the Lover of Horses. And Philip was not ignorant of the power of this native weapon and its superiority over iron. 'There is no city I cannot get into in Greece if I send a few of my Philips in front of me,' he is said to have remarked. Like all real realists he had no penchant for violence and no illusions about its limitations. If you have the power to buy, it is always better to buy than to force. Such a man is in the new royal line of Tyrants for one of the earliest of these had laid down as that dynasty's maxim: 'Wars are bad for Tyrannies.' So Philip did not so much conquer Greece as offer her his services. He saw this was to be not a conquest but a union, for each had much to gain from the other and much that by themselves they could not provide. He could forge an ample corselet for the shining Greek mind, that was lying like a snake that has cast its skin and cannot grow another. And the Greek mind could inform and inspire with creative originality the state he could frame. As a supreme diplomatist he came as a suppliant. He would ask them to give him a step up in the world. He would request that they should establish his status as one of themselves, make clear he was a cousin, country if you will, but no barbarian, with the proper sense that marks every civilised man of the city's superiority. So he obtains the right of entry of his chariots for the Greek games, as no barbarian was permitted to have a chariot entered. This is his patent of civilisation. Nor is there any reason to suppose this was a cynical stoop. He was by birth and taste a country Greek, and though he could see how highbrows were imperilling their great culture, that did not make him despise it, but rather resolved him to save it. He had gold and armies. He might have conquered the north and had an empire cheap: or spoiled straight away Persia and had loot. But he was not a raider. He was the practical complement of the Greek enquiring mind. He had to combine with it to make something new. And to create that new thing – a cultured and scientific state as powerful in the world of men and as secure, as it was enterprising and brave in the world of Nature – to that he gave his genius. For this reason King Philip is a figure of such significance. Assassination cut short his career and gave the instruments he had forged into hands as capable but a mind as romantic as Philip's, his father's, had been realist.

Greece was bound to undergo a unification. The little states which had sunk sociologically almost to the level of limited liability companies (where at the shareholders' meeting should one be dissatisfied with his share he would withdraw his capital) were bound to be crushed by a power composed of a more massive loyalty. Greece was fortunate in her conqueror for she could accept him as a partner – one whom she had to obey but whom also she could teach. Her self-respect was thus salved and the

conquest accepted, and had Philip lived there seems
no reason why there should have been the revolt of
Thebes and so no reason to ask whether he would
have suppressed it with the neurotic savagery of his
son. Alexander's genius makes far more stir than
advance. He uses the inventions Philip had made
not for fresh inventions but cashes them out. A
power which should have been used to brace and
buttress the Greek genius so that in Hellas there
might be raised higher than ever before, secure
against the attacks of lower organisations, a civilisation artistic, scientific, humanitarian, was expended
rushing aimlessly along on ground level. It ran
right through the hollow Persian Empire and dived
deep into India, but it was in itself as uncreative as
an aerolite. No doubt many spores of Greek culture
were carried in its wake and sprouted later along its
path. But the task of Greece was not to export her
styles but to advance her own thought: it was really
as little use to make barbarians look like Hellenes
as it is to put an Australian black in a top hat. At
the base, in Hellas itself, no solution was being
found to the universal problems the Greek mind had
raised. Alexander was exporting, not solutions but
riddles, not a new integrative force but dissolutive
ideas. He himself could only offer the world a crude
form of military autocracy, as sterilising to the
political sense of the 'orientals' on which it descended
as it was irrelevant to the social problems the Greeks
had failed to solve, and Philip had taken the first

step to solve. That Greece might have gone on if
Philip had lived, that the Macedonian graft was
sound and the Greek spirit could recruit itself from
the Macedonian hinterland, there can be no doubt.
For from Stageira, a Macedonian townlet, came the
supreme Greek genius. Socrates could analyse away
superstition and prejudice. Plato could dream of the
perfect state the cities should be and never would
be. But with Aristotle we find at last a fully modern
mind. Here instead of logomacy and myths we get
the first and basic attempt to make an entire system
of knowledge which may find place and use for all
the new experience which the newly emerged
critical faculty has found. He is a culmination.
Thought had made a system of abstractions with
which the new objective world could be handled.
In the great sixth century, on the geographical
bound of Greek expansion, Pythagoras in South
Italy had discovered the abstract concept of number
and laid the foundation of a complete arithmetic on
that base. Aristotle himself was to raise the first
stage of mathematics by the concept of Infinity –
the idea that as number is an abstraction, is something the mind of man has made, so man may divide
and multiply as far as he will. With mathematics
and 'natural history' – the catalogue of phenomena
– man could frame a complete scientific system of
the world, by order, comparison and measurement.
All was prepared on the side of thought. The
philosophers had brought their side of the task to

a condition when a complete half of experience was ordered. It now needed a junction to be effected with the other side, the side of practical statesman-like policy, with sociality and morality. Without that junction further advance could not be made. That junction effected, the present advance was secured and the future advance, infinitely greater, guaranteed. The world of thought waited on the world of action. It waited in vain. Philip might have been a philosopher king, one who would have used all knowledge to set ever stronger and freer the mind of man; a ruler who would have put back into the business of living, ever better and knowing, ever more fully, all the new resources and faculties that natural philosophy yielded. Certainly Alexander was not – he was only a hero – at that date an atavism.[1] Plato went off to make a philosopher king in Sicily, but neither the philosopher nor the king knew their common business and the poor old poetical mathematician returned disheartened. Aristotle and Philip is a much more promising combination – *sed dis aliter visum*.

III

So, failing the junction of the two forces, their unification into a homogeneous whole, a fully

---

[1] E.g. His abominable 'traditional' treatment of the Governor of Gizah.

philosophical polity wherein the full scientific knowledge of man should be completely used and
reciprocated by a fully scientific community, there
had to be retreat. Science cannot be sustained, far
less persisted in and advanced, if the state persists in
remaining sub-scientific. Whether revolutions have
or have not any 'need of chemists,' it is certain that
militarisms can have no use or place for philosophers.
It is therefore not hard to understand that Aristotle
marks a high watermark, and that in his own
Academy he is followed only by commentators.
It is enough for his successors if they can understand
what it was the master had talked about. They
could at best only, along his workings, get up to the
face of the seam on which he was engaged. Once
that piercing intellect was gone they could only
gaze, with wonder at the passages it had cut, with
despair at the rock face of reality that confronted
them and on which their feeble penetrative powers
made no mark.

Such is the state of mind at the close of the fourth
century in Greece. Alexander is dead and his
empire has lasted no longer than will last the
empires of the other heroes, Attila, Ghenghis,
Timour. His generals finding themselves stranded
over a sub-continent, try to dig themselves in.
Ptolemy in the natural enclave of Egypt is most
happy as to terrain and most subtle in realising his
social position. Though a simple Macedonian,
whose culture had it grown must have made him a

Hellene, he adapts himself to Egyptian custom with such success that not only does he himself become a Pharaoh and his house one of the Dynasties, but his house persists and persists successfully through the custom, natural in Egypt but horrifying to a European, of brother and sister marriages. However disconcerting to northern morality, that the custom was not *unnatural* is proved by the fact that, three centuries after, the Ptolemaic stock is vigorous enough to throw up a woman who played for the world with Cæsar as her partner, and but for his death might have won. North of Ptolemy the Seleucidæ had a far less formidable position, and one they managed with far less skill. Instead of becoming Syrianised, as Ptolemy had become Egyptianised, they insisted on exhibiting a superficial Hellenism that was as false in spirit as it was inapposite in display. A danger spot in their new prosperity was Judea. The Jewish people, eroded by tolerance and disintegrated by the individualistic speculations of the age, was looking for some occasion that might once again brace them together and close their ranks. Antiochus Epiphanes played into their hands. Insisting upon an adoption of Greek forms, in denial of the Greek spirit, at a stroke he undid all the work of Cyrus, and Jewish nationalism appeared again, revived to be a thorn in the side of empire for the next three hundred years. But the spirit of nationalist defiance awoken in Palestine appears nowhere else. Through the large district of Asia Minor only family dynastic quarrels appear to disturb the indifference of humanity. The enthusiasm of the ordinary man went not into nationalistic politics or scientific philosophy but increasingly into the Mystery Religions. Here in secret excitements, ecstatic states, initiations, illusions and dreams of another life, men, who tired of hard and aimless living, found increasingly their refuge. In Greece, too, in spite of the fact that the feebleness of the Macedonian house encouraged revolt and provoked the last flicker of the old local patriotisms, the Mystery cult spread. The best men were to become devoted and largely absorbed by these other worldly exercises. Political life, which had once been the study and glory of Hellas was now reduced, however often romantic rebellion flared for a moment, to adulations offered to the Macedonian Tyrant as though he were a saviour god able to give his worshippers luck here and salvation hereafter. In brief the ancient world is getting emptier and emptier and its life beats ever more faintly. The highway of East and West which Persia had opened and across which Alexander had progressed now becomes blocked. The Parthians, a cavalry people more rudimentary than the Macedonians, descend on Persia. Here they find shards of Hellenism but without a spark of the fire they once carried. So the spoilers lie like an avalanche blocking the intercourse of the continents. In Cyprus, between the Jewish experiment in social righteousness, the

Egyptian experiment in individual holiness and the Greek experiment in critical enquiry, appears Zeno, the founder of Stoicism. He is of Syrian stock. In him blend the Near East and the Near West, brought together in a common disillusionment. It is with his system that philosophy definitely changes from free, impersonal enquiry into the nature of the Universe, into a sanctionless, purely ethical religion. Philosophy ceases to be Science regardless of consequences, and becomes a spiritual exercise in order to save the individual from circumstances. The emergent mind of man has gone as far as it may unsupported by an adequate and congruent polity. As the state would not guarantee and secure that advance, the individual had to devote all his energies to such discoveries as would give him the immunity the state failed to provide. Whether this was good for the individual it was certainly fatal to the state. Only one state protected philosophers in the pursuit of the original scientific aims of philosophy, and that was the strange State of the Ptolemies. Cynically able to become incestuous Pharaohs, they were also able, being at heart far more Greek than their royal connections, the Seleucidæ, to patronise natural enquiry. In consequence Alexandria carries on the expansion of scientific knowledge that had begun in Ionia and echoed as far as Calabria, had crossed on to Cos, Samos and the other islands of the Ægean and had landed for a little while on Greece. Geometry becomes a complete technique with Euclid, and this new instrument helps to measure the earth and estimate the stars. Science was on the brink of becoming practical politics. The Pharos, the lighthouse that was one of the Wonders of the World, may have been equipped with condensing mirrors. The steam engine may have been glimpsed. Even as late as A.D. 50, when the Ptolemies had vanished, sparks of science still remained, and Hero's Ælipile invented at that date, was a steam instrument that pointed straight to the steam engine. No doubt the men of that age never suspected that they had reached the top of the pass – a step more and the path would slope down, discovery leading to discovery, power begetting fresh power. We can see an Egypt, made by Greek Fire, and perhaps even gunpowder, impregnable, and so within its frontiers safely able by unstinted invention to raise itself to a standard of wealth, security and understanding never attained by civilisation until our nineteenth century. Here philosophers, if they had not been kings, would have been peers, the recognised aristocracy, and as they kept to natural science and avoided the premature synthesis of Stoicism, even under the moderate freedom given them by the despotic Ptolemies, there seems no reason why as their powers grew they should have abandoned the love of pure Science and shrunk back into Ethics. But the moment passed; further, royal support was not forthcoming. The advanced pioneers slipped back. The ground was lost: the pass towered above. The promised land of scientific security and plenty remained unentered. It is still to be firmly occupied to-day. The people wander not 40 years, not 400, but 2300, waiting still the philosopher king, or the philosophic order, which shall lead them in.

In one other place the last wave of speculation – long locked and laid at its source – still rolls toward the sunset. Greece now has only ears for philosophy that will tell it about individual preservation and escape. But in Magna Græcia the old passion to understand still glimmers. In the third century Archimedes in Sicily is still advancing pure mathematics, still interested in making discoveries and inventions, still able to make abstractions and so able, as the experiment with the crown of Dionysis showed, still to make the most surprising discoveries. It is fitting that this man, who with his practical science may actually have helped his little city-state to resist the Romans, should have died at their hands as they took and extinguished the city-state life of his Syracuse. The story of his end, struck dead by a looting soldier as he, unaware of the end, brooded with complete abstraction over a mathematical problem, may not be true of the individual man, but it is true of the spirit which for the last time for sixteen hundred years shone out in him upon Europeans. Society had failed to support the philosopher, to complement his findings; so the society, in which philosophers could appear, vanished and a cruder one, that would not live beyond its spiritual means or speculate beyond its power of achievement, had to take its place.

CHAPTER X

THE EMPIRE OF IRON AND CLAY

I

THE Macedonian Empire was Hellenic in form, and almost became Hellenic in spirit. The Roman Empire was a cruder affair and was content with a few Greek ornaments. The instrument of the Roman legion pierced the whole hollow Mediterranean world even more thoroughly than had the Macedonian phalanx pierced the Persian Empire.

Again the middle man of civilisation manages to make himself master. For Italy, as before was Macedonia, is now the frontier between civilised societies, subtle, resourceful, but weak with self-consciousness, and barbarian tribes, resolute and

violent, but unorganised, ill-equipped and desperate.
So easily can Rome learn to divide and rule.
On one side the barbarians cannot stand before
her scientific organisation and equipment, on the
other the civilisations cannot stand before her
savage bravery and will to conquer. Yet Rome has
no message to give the world as had Persia and as
had Macedonia borrowed from Hellas. The Roman
Empire is therefore far more an accident, an event
not shaped by the doer but forced upon him by
circumstances, than are the two earlier empires.
It finds, too, a world more grown up than they
found. The idea of the city-state was everywhere, and
on the top of that was the idea of the self-respecting
and even self-cherishing individual, that Stoicism
was sowing far and wide. Nor could Rome get at
the spiritual lives of the simpler less philosophic folk
for they were finding secret escapes into another
world through the Mystery Religions. So the Roman
Empire, as no rule before, had to be rational,
utilitarian: a coercion or a convenience; it could not
be a uniting spirit. In brief, it had to come to terms
with individuality. The Roman Empire has three
distinct phases when it is still in the ascendent. First,
it is simply conquest. A group of people with the
ordinary simple agricultural gods and notions about
life discover that they can conquer. After achieving
a base broad enough for full scale strategy, they come
up against Carthage, a power strong enough to
test them, to make them become completely

militarised in the effort and to yield them as their prize of conquest a span of the Mediterranean. There follows a period of expansion and exploitation. This second stage is made possible by three things: Carthage had drawn Rome on to the sea. Lack of sea power finally decreed the limits of the Persian Empire. For it the last ditch was the Ægean. Xerxes has his army accompanied by the fleet (lost afterwards in Salamis Bay), but his whole strategy is conceived in terms of an army marched round by land. So, too, the Macedonian Empire is made by a series of land campaigns. But when the 'power belt' (that decisive district between the unorganised savage and the disheartened civilised, whence conquerors and empire builders must always spring) lies no longer between the steppe and the shore lands, but on a peninsular, then its people must win the sea if they are to win empire. This Carthage taught Rome to do, and this was a new step. Up till then sea power had been an antithesis instead of the complement of land power. The great nations and the empires were based on land masses and only used fleets defensively, to beat off attacks on their coasts. The most successful empire was therefore the empire which exposed least coast and all expansion was away from the sea inland. The idea of holding open the sea and making it a highway was foreign to the first civilisations. To them it must be, not a way, but the final barrier – the outermost thing – the dark moat that shuts in the castle of the world and so a place, not where civilisation might spread but where outlawry and piracy alone could endure. The first people to make the sea part of their polity and livelihood were therefore the pirates who were in time to become merchants. They did not think in terms of a civilisation patiently stored up by a slow agricultural yield. They thought in terms of adventure, exchange, the opening of new markets, new traffic, new routes. So Crete builds up her plutocracy, and after her collapse the Phœnicians show that the new polity can be practised not only from an island (such for example as Samos), but from the mainland shore, provided the mind always looked out on the sea as its true base and on the land as no more than a link, a point of support. Avoiding 'entangling alliances' with the elder mainland agricultural polity, helped to keep touch and yet to keep detached, through the invention of money, the Phœnicians built up a wealth more condensed and mobile than the world had so far seen. And the adventurous, enterprising life – the distances a man might explore by sea – made them conversant with strangeness, opened still further their minds and stimulated them to improve all methods of exchange. So they make money more current, advance calculation and improve the alphabet – for all these things are necessary for fuller and wider trade. But above all are they sea-minded. They have taken the plunge and to them it is the land that is deep and dangerous, the sea wide and friendly and their native ground. So though they touch the coast and plant their stations and factories, these are carefully circumscribed. Their settlements are only bridge heads through which to draw from the elder cultures supplies, and steps to lead the explorers into wider seas. Carthage was one such out-station left to grow independently after Alexander had destroyed the original Phœnician base. It kept up the tradition of exploration, for its admiral Hanno made the classic voyage down the outer African coast and brought back the skin of the gorilla. But though the western waters of the Mediterranean were the true base of Carthaginian power, African Carthage having its complement in Spanish Carthage, these and a dozen other trading cities being as it were the bastions of a city floored with the sea and whose wall was the breakers, yet Carthage was not without rivals. Its territory was interpenetrated by Greek cities and routes. Sicily was central in the polity, and Sicily was far more Greek than Phœnician, while South Italy was Magna Græcia and even the Gaulish coast had on it Greek cities on the sites of Marseilles and Toulon. Carthage therefore was drawn into local wars, and as she did not conquer the Italian peninsular, that large 'reentrant angle' of land thrust into her sea – Italy had to conquer her and in conquering her to succeed to her sea kingdom.

The first thing then that makes the Roman Empire an advance on the three earlier empires –

the Egyptian, Persian and Macedonian – is the combination of sea with land power. The second thing was the possession of a new military weapon. Epaminondas had transformed the phalanx from an ordinary line of pike men into a single weapon which a strategist could poise, aim and launch with instantaneous and irresistible effect. Philip had practised and enlarged this weapon until no other army could stand before it. But it had the faults of its virtues. Like all heavy armament, though able to smash through anything that should withstand it, it lacked flexibility. Though the Romans are thought of as inflexible their supreme invention was to give a new flexibility to arms. Almost as soon as Rome had crushed Carthage and succeeded to the sea she was threatened from the other side, from the mainland. The Gauls were again gathering from the wide north lands to descend on the peninsular. It was another of those periodic flockings of nomadic barbarians; but this one rushed south when the settled farming stock were quite ready to hit back. The Gauls were not to repeat the victory their Brennus had earlier inflicted on Rome. The genius of Marius annihilates that danger and the instrument with which he slaughtered the myriads of barbarians in his great victory in Provence was the legion – a phalanx made complex and flexible. This instrument shortly afterwards had to face the elder Macedonian phalanx. The general, Flamininus, who was given it to handle, understood his instru-

ment. At Cynoscephalæ he manœuvred the Macedonian phalanx on to broken ground. The irregular
surface made the too rigid ranking open and crack.
The legion with its more flexible organisation kept
its shape, struck home, and from then till the use of
the armoured cavalry and bow in the Middle Ages
the fate of nations will not be influenced by the
discovery of a new offensive weapon, though as we
shall see the ancient world will add, late in its day,
one very important element, fire, to its defensive.

We can therefore turn to the third factor that
made the Roman Empire. That was raw wealth.
The resources of the world had been steadily
mounting. The Phœnician trade had linked up all
the commerce of the Mediterranean. The ancient
world was now a single market, and now a single
authority was able to take the entire toll. For a
while Rome was content to take all the traffic
would bear, and outside opposition, such as the
gallant effort of Mithradates in Pontus, was no more
than enough to stimulate the legions to continue
their conquests and teach the generals how to
operate on such distant fronts. But Rome itself was
no longer, and could not be any longer, a unit. The
bankers – the 'Knights' – had made immensely out
of the conquests, but the people were poor. Money
was once again having its way and to him that had
it was given all else, lands and homes and labour,
and from him that had it not, inevitably melted
away even the little holding which had seemed so

inalienably his, even his personal freedom. Rome
itself was therefore breaking up – it was being
disrupted by its conquests. The old homogeneous
resolution is gone. Sure symptom of this, the old
religio – the pious and satisfying performance of
antique state rites – is neglected, and personal
religion – the religion of otherworldliness and com-
pensatory promises of an after life – the religion of
the Mysteries, begins to appear. More and more
men (the underlings who have been crushed, the
over-men who have had to look on and in their
detachment have had to ask why others were thrown
under and they thrown up) question the rightness
of things as they are. From both ends of the social
scale the revolution in Religion, that revolution to
a personal private religion which we have seen
working centuries before in the older societies,
begins now to affect the latest Empire. The very
force which gave Rome its final irresistibility, money
power, seemed to be about to prove the force which
would end by dissolving the enormous state almost
as soon as it was formed.

II

Rome, however, was to last some centuries. The
truth is that societies learn, as well as individuals.
Roman society did not succumb instantaneously to
the disintegrative social disease. The organism had
evidently learnt somehow and to some extent to

react to this disintegration of social unity, and, what it brought in its train, the invasion of discouragement and doubt. The answer was Roman Law, Roman citizenship, the Imperial Principate, and the centralising of authority in the hands of this one person by his direct control of the legions.

Here, too, we may see an idea adopted probably unconsciously from the Tyrants. The army, the sanction of law and order, is no longer the people in arms to defend their laws and boundaries. It is the detached instrument of a single human being's will. In the later Empire, as the legions are recruited increasingly on the spot and are not moved, a regional feeling grows up and this aids the Empire's disintegration. But at the beginning of the Empire this spirit did not stir. The will of the people is gone. In its stead is the wish of millions of individuals for quiet and security, to be allowed to leave public concerns alone and to get along with the satisfaction of their appetites or the salvation of their souls. This the Principate, with all its faults, provided, until men became at length even too listless to give it the little support it required. The tragedy of the Roman Empire is not due to military decadence: on the contrary, as Dr. Collingwood has shown, the men who handled the instrument probably went on throughout the period of its use, gaining in efficiency. If Rome suffered from military troubles the fault was one of excess. Outwardly it was always a military dictatorship and this character increased with age. Nor is the collapse to be attributed to economic breakdown. It is true the monetary system, the taxation and the whole of the finance were absurdly inadequate for the huge continental system they were supposed to keep running. But as Dr. Heitland pointed out, the Greek freedmen who increasingly ran the administration, had devised a system of exchequer, accounts and calculation that was an invention in bureaucracy. It seems that as in the army, so in the civil service there was quite a considerable amount of new devices framed to deal with the unprecedented circumstances. In fact, it is increasingly clear that had the ordinary citizen wanted the Empire to go on, on it would have gone. It was clumsy and oppressive, it ground and stuck, because he did not care enough that it should run well. For the real concern of the ordinary intelligent citizen of the mid-Roman Empire is not statesmanship but religion, not an efficient world here, but a blessed world hereafter. The Roman Empire must last its time. As an instrument it cannot be broken. The forces without must wait till the weapon falls from the imperial hand. But generation after generation the paralysis spreads, the disintegration interpenetrates. The Mystery Religions had sapped the citizenship of the men of the Greek city-states. The practice of these cults, which gave an ecstasy which obliterated the present and enforced a doctrine which made the future otherworldly, spread all over the Roman Empire as a virus is carried by the circulation throughout the body. Even the legions had their own Mystery, Mithraism, which though it approved the military values, found – as an individualised age must find – that their ultimate sanction was not here but in another life. And then, when saturation point was reached, the revolution took place, the body was transformed. The real crisis of the ancient world is not when the legions are withdrawn from the frontiers or when a puppet Emperor, such as Romulus Augustulus, is put aside and people see what they have always known, that Odovacer, the barbarian, is really ruling. It is when, in 313, the Empire has openly to acknowledge that it cannot crush an organised Mystery Religion, which not only draws men from their interest in this world, but actually refuses to permit them to make outward affirmation of their citizenship and loyalty to the State.[1] The legion had no rival, but against this spiritual force it was helpless. Rome fell when it fell under the protection[2] of Christianity. That of course, is not to say that Christianity was a mistake or a tragedy, still less a 'triumph of barbarism and religion.' It is simply to

[1] The Roman Empire tolerated any religion but would not and could not permit secret societies. This the Christians insisted on being. That, and the fact that they refused to take the oath to the Emperor, and that an unbroken succession of Fathers down to Lactantuis had denounced military service as impossible for a Christian, explain sufficiently their persecution by the State, and how significant was its capitulation to them.

[2] Christ is styled as had been Mithra, the Protector of the Empire. So the Mystery God of the Legions is replaced by that of a more other-worldly order.

record the fact that men who were convinced that all sanctions of conduct resided in another world to be entered after death (and eternal happiness in which depended on a life of abstinence) had taken over authority from men who had held the one sanction to be military force. This must mean a recasting of life because of a reorientation of interest. The centre of gravity of human concerns has shifted until even the state must appear, if it is to save itself at all, to be otherworldly, a projection from the other side shaped and authorised by powers into whose presence the individual only comes after death. The emperor sinks to be a vicegerent. His legions are helpless against the new power. He receives back his authority but not even as a vicar, only as a curate. It is not hard, therefore, to understand why a realist of the calibre of Constantine – who saw the necessity of obtaining this new lease, and so won against his less realistic rivals who failed to estimate the shift to imponderables – could listen hour by hour to the metaphysical wranglings of the Councils. He knew with the intuitive sense of the cynical statesman that he was up against a new crystallisation of force, and he would spare no time necessary to study it. Anxiously he watched whether it was assuaged, whether it would stick to its terms, whether he had stabilised the front, checked the social rot, or whether his concordat was in vain and the spiritual heads could not deliver back to him the loyalty and energy of his subjects. Certainly he is one of the world's great statesmen. In the days of his power he cared only for power.[1] He fought a masterly action to save that power and to preserve the Empire. But it was not a victory, only a rear action. The tide in the affairs of men was against him, and though he might buy the bishops and they might hand over their flocks to be his soldiers, the bishops themselves could not deliver the goods. Whether the bishops personally wished it or not, the Roman civilisation was becoming so individualised, and therefore so clearly aware that moral sanctions could only be found in a spiritual post-obit world, that that civilisation was bound to demand that it be ruled, if ruled at all, not by a soldier but by a magician. The Roman Emperor had, in his absorption with military control, allowed to slip into the background his mystic title of Pontifex Maximus, the great priest who links the living with the dead. So the Bishop of the Imperial See was to pick up that title and in its right rule for the next thousand years the civilisation of Europe, West Central.

---

[1] *N.B.* – His deathbed baptism with the words, 'Now let there be no doubt.' Till then he had been playing at religion to save the Empire, now he was caught by religion and only wished to save his soul.

CHAPTER XI

ADVANCE ON THE OUTSKIRTS, AND THE
RE-EMERGENCE OF EUROPE

I.

AT this point when Europe was, as we shall see, about
to decline into the shade and the progress of man's
mind was for some centuries to be advanced solely
by Asiatics, we may turn a moment from the front.
We may cease for a space to watch the still rising
crest of the fountain of knowledge and glance over
the world to see how the waves of thought, that

221

sprung from the three original river-valley societies, are spreading round the globe.

China has already been mentioned, as a cultural centre that responded to the revolutionary moral movement in the seventh century B.C. But though China, with Confucius and Lao Tze so early contributed to the thought of civilisation, China is not one of civilisation's sources. Of that there can be no doubt, for China lies too far north. The three elder river-valley societies must have had a start of at least a thousand years before the far more northerly land of the Yellow River was habitable. We also know that the Mongolian skin is, of all human skins, the one most adapted to cold. We can therefore conclude that this great people had to force their way on the heels of the Ice into what was not for centuries to become the Flowery Land. Finally, as evidence that China is an offshoot of the central civilisation, the earliest settlements of the Mongolian stock known in China are up in the extreme westerly entrances of the country. There can be no doubt that the Mongols spread in from the West and at no very early date, for the earliest of these settlements found is about 1700 B.C. As late as Confucius the land is still divided among kinglets, and a feudal system rather than an empire is the next stage of China's organisation. Later, China was to take part, and an honourable part, in the creation and exchange of ideas and inventions. We have noted the influence of Confucius, but it was an influence which was not felt outside Asia until the Jesuit missionaries made known his thought to the West. But beside ideas of government and morality, China pretty certainly originated printing and gunpowder, and both of these inventions may have been carried West long before Chinese thought on social theory. China herself was too conservative to exploit either of these finds. Neither original in civilisation nor daring in its application, China never pushed to an extreme any of its powers, but was constantly falling in love with her past achievement, and so failing to see any lure in the future. Her printing was apparently evolved from seals. These were used largely for stamping charms. Gradually it became necessary to alter the charm a little to fit the particular case. A seal set with a curse to blight cattle might be made so that the sign for cattle could be slipped out, and the sign for crops slipped in. Gradually block printing of an elaborate and delicate beauty was evolved. But printing proper was not natural to a people whose writing had stuck at ideographs, and who had refused to move on to the rational and convenient abstraction of an alphabet. So the Chinese idea had to go West till it found a people with this complementary power. There can be little doubt that this is one of the true and perhaps the most important migrations of an invention in the ancient world. The steps are still to be traced out, but when we realise that a Koran was printed in Cairo in the thirteenth century with movable type, we can at least see that it is going to prove more and more difficult to believe that Europe discovered printing on its own. We have mentioned gunpowder and the Chinese failure to use it for defence. Exploration, however, they did more to advance than either the Greeks or the Phœnicians, for it seems that they struck on the loadstone and so came by the first crude compass.

If it is true of great China with all its later contributions to culture, that is it nevertheless an offshoot of civilisation, even more is this true of all the other sprays of culture that we find farther afield. Three such have become famous. First, of course, is that of Japan, but it need not detain us, for however remarkable in its consistency, it is even less remarkable in its originality than China – for from China it drew with a patient and devout imitativeness all its culture. So Japan is two degrees removed from creativeness. Finally there are the two strangest and furthest shoots – the Aztec-Maya and the Inca cultures, shining so faintly and so far in the night of history that, like Neptune and Pluto, they seem hardly to belong to our system.

Set so far afield, they seem to have developed a curiously disproportionate and unbalanced culture. Indeed, that seems their peculiar interest. Their equipment, the general level of their powers and culture on which they reared their civilisation was curiously rudimentary. In some ways it was only a Stone Age culture. They seem to have carved their complicated stone steles with nothing but stone, and they built their pyramids and temples with no knowledge of vault or arch, using for their spans ingenious corbelling and lamination. And perhaps most startling of their cultural lacunæ, though they united great districts, they never invented the wheel. Indeed, throughout they seem to show great ingenuity in developing a few crude ideas which they had inherited, but to which they could add nothing basic. The Incas with such a simple inheritance made a complete, fast-locked culture. They are perhaps the most perfect example of a society which, with a drastic restriction of ideas, organises itself as an entirety and with finality. The whole of society was so completely articulated that it was, at its height – as so completely articulated a social unit must be – a perfect socialism and also a perfect caste system. All the knowledge it had was perfectly exploited. In spite of ignorance of the wheel, an ignorance that must have starved transport, great works of communication were carried out so that the whole state might be in constant touch. The classes were rigidly fixed, yet all were looked after, even as the hand which must never dare think for itself is constantly thought for by the brain whose orders it unquestioningly carries out. This strange segregated seed of culture thus developed its full capacity. It attained a completely classicised culture. Then suddenly it was brought up against disease, treachery, violence, originality. Before such a blast of invasion the kingdom of the Incas broke and vanished as a Prince Rupert's Drop breaks and vanishes the moment it is cracked.

The culture of the Maya was hardly less strange. It, too, had from a stone age base and equipment raised a civilisation that was at least in one respect as advanced as any at that date throughout the world. It seems from the dating of its steles that somewhere between 200 B.C. and A.D. 200 – the period when as it happens not only was the Roman Empire expanding over the Western world, but China too was attaining a maximum of expansion with the Han Empire, that spread from the Pacific to the Caspian – the Maya reached the height of their culture and brought to a curious perfection their special study, Astronomy. Here was a people who had discovered for themselves all the mathematical basis requisite for considerable applied science, and yet they seem never to have applied it. The whole social structure seems to have existed to carry the numerous priestly-astronomer class whose sole duty appears to have been to scan the sky and every four years to meet in immense conclave 'to put Pop right,' *i.e.* to calculate for the leap year and to correct the calendar – a vivid example of the disproportionate development of their social system. For this culture was so inept in spite of its pure knowledge that it was in ruin before the Spaniards touched it. The great cities had been deserted some centuries earlier. The most likely reason for this seems to be that their agriculture had remained so primitive that their maze farming had completely exhausted the ground that was open for cultivation, and such was the rudimentariness of their tools that they could not clear fresh gound from the forest and keep it clear. A people who were real star-gazers starved because of their ignorance of the earth on which they had to live or die.

So we see that the furthest limits of the radiation that is civilisation did produce a glimmer of authentic light, but that it did not illuminate far the Natural World that lay about man, and even that glimmer soon died. Outside these spots the nomad and the savage wander and camp. Civilisation is one and until our own day it has never made good for more than a few centuries anywhere far outside the great Eurasian bloc. We can therefore return to the centre and see how there, whence the light radiates, men were striving to make it still brighter.

II

We had reached in our survey the rise and dominance of the Papacy and the decline of the Roman Principate. The centuries that stretch immediately beyond this seem, therefore, because Mediterranean man, through whom civilisation had for centuries been working, has definitely adopted a 'magical' and 'otherworldly' view, to be centuries of declining light. But that is largely because we

227

either continue to fix our eyes where the light was first detected in Greece and Magna Græcia, or, with even poorer vision, we fix them on our own northern countries and impatiently await the appearance of the enlightenment in these barren hinterlands. It is true that West Central Europe lost its place as a centre, if not a part, of civilisation, and those northern lands such as Britain, which had been feebly illumined by Rome's reflection of Greek thought, sank back into a twilight of the mind. But the mind of man was continuing to struggle, to emerge and free itself from circumstance. We have seen that the Alexandrian scientific explorations and finds certainly went on as late as the first century A.D., and this front of discovery we can detect running north and east from Egypt. Indeed, there is increasing reason to suppose that had we an adequate history of the Middle East we should find that it is here at this epoch that the mind of man crested and the thought of civilisation was preserved and even augmented. We have but fragments with which to estimate this age, but they are highly suggestive. The Romans claimed but one art, architecture. It used to seem that they took building, which the Greek had made too purely an æsthetic, and even a mathematic, exercise, and made it an applied art. They took the Hellenic temple and introduced huge vaults and apses and a building which had been a crystallisation in stone of a structure originally wooden, they transformed by the use of concrete.

But now it seems that this use of the dome in square building is not a contribution from the West, but from the East.[1] Syria it was that experienced the meeting of East and West, and it was here the domical construction, practised in Mesopotamia for 3000 years, was blended with the Greek outline. So classic building is a Syrian invention. During the same time and in the same place we know glass making, which is a very practical approach to chemistry, was being practised, and the world-famous glass mosaics, put up in the early eighth century in Damascus, we can now judge for ourselves, obviously have behind them a great tradition of artistic vigour. Is it not in this quarter then that we should look for the rise of that art which till now we have thought Byzantine? The Mohammedan destruction of all representations of men or animals would have obliterated in their land of origin these records. It is not surprising, therefore, to find 'the fertile crescent' (the rim of country that runs from Palestine through Syria, connects across by Aleppo, Homs and Palmyra to Mesopotamia and so down to Seleucis and Ctesiphon) bearing intellectual fruits. For this rim of country is now once again a frontier between a too active and turbulent barbarism and a too passive and disheartened civilisation, and such frontiers and crosses, we have seen, are always mentally fertile. On the western side is the exhausted Levant, on the northern the turbulent

[1] See Lethaby and Swainson, *Hagia Sophia*.

uplands. The Parthian power is still mainly a chivalry and is just about to be overthrown by the revolt of the original Persian stock under the Sassanidæ. The Roman power has repeatedly tried to push back the Persian but the Persian more than holds his own, and it is with difficulty that Rome can reassert its hold on Syria. It is not unnatural that in the cities of Mesopotamia, once the cradle of civilisation, Greek philosophy is preserved and the tradition of Greek speculation and experimentation carried on. So strongly indeed is this kindled that, when from the desert to the south of it the great gale of Mohammedan enthusiastic conquest sweeps out on the world, the light is not put out but, on the contrary, brands are sent whirling as far as the Atlantic, India, and the highlands of Persia; scientific thought is kindled in Spain and fanned by the Indus, and beacon answers to beacon. This opening up again of communications between greater Asia and Europe was important. For India has been following her own course in the development of civilisation. She, too, had had her age of matriarchy, her Heroic age,[1] and we know that she must have had her first age of Science somewhere about the same time as the Hellenic because it was about the beginning of the Christian era – when Hero was making his steam experiments in Alexandria – that in India that great step in mathematical

[1] Cf. *The Heroic Age in India: a Comparative Study*, Prof. N. K. Sidhanta, 'History of Civilisation Series.'

abstraction, the invention of Zero, was made; to be followed shortly after by the further exploration of the unknown, by the invention of negative numbers. The opening up of the world to one cultural circulation from the Pyrenees to the Punjab allowed therefore an advance of thought so that not only were the Greek classics preserved, but mathematics, astronomy and chemistry were advanced.

Why, therefore, did not this higher and more practical civilisation prevail against Europe and the European religion disappear before a second attack of simplifying desert moral theology, as the Olympian deities, varied, iridescent, but of doubtful illuminative value, had vanished before the earlier Hebraic invasion? One practical reason is found in a last flash of Greek inventiveness. That Hellenistic Syria which is, it seems, the source of classical architecture and industrial chemistry, produced also in its chemical experiments Greek Fire. On the side of the offensive powers of man nothing had been added to the legion. As has been said, the knight in armour is the next advance. But to defensive armament an immense addition was made by this flame weapon. The defences of such a fort of fortresses as Constantinople were worked out with perfect skill. The danger of rigid defences is that the attacker can choose his point. With true engineering science not only could every point be defended by a cross fire, but such a fire could be made annihilating. Indeed, there was only one weakness in such a defence. It was so adequate that it could completely exhaust its munitions. So the invention of a new weapon that could be manufactured and stored in great quantities put the last touch to Constantinople's impregnability. Not till gunpowder supersedes Greek fire and artillery can reply to the flame-caster, not for another thousand years, will Constantinople pass for good out of the Greek hands and Mohammedanism at last, and too late, clear this bulwark from its path.

Greek Fire, a produce of late Greek invention, was the occasion that checked Mohammedanism. For several centuries the Greeks had been feeling their way toward some such weapon but it was not till the very generation in which Mohammedanism erupted in Arabia that, through the chemical skill of the architect Callinicus, who came from Heliopolis in Syria, the Greek Fire was brought to the full pitch of its efficiency. Probably a mixture of sulphur, naphtha, and quicklime, it had the disconcerting property of catching fire when it touched water, and against this the real Wild-fire, the hottest enthusiasm of fanaticism was helpless. It illustrates how no weakness of civilisation need yield it a prey to more military nations if only it keep hold of Science, and let understanding make up for lack of force. A perfectly scientific state must always be impregnable. But though Greek Fire singed off the Arab swarm that would have looted the capital of the Christian world, why was not Christendom taken in the flank? Spain fell at a blow – why not Gaul, and so Italy and Rome, then the Balkan Peninsula, and so Byzantium be left isolated, a capital without an Empire? The Mohammedan forces were, however, overthrown at Tours by Martel, and after that the West Moorish wing is never again an imminent peril. It would seem that as the Persian Empire was at the end of its tether when it grappled with the Greeks, so Mohammedanism was too far from its base when it attacked the Franks. Also, and this is perhaps even more important, its first enthusiasm was spent. The original crusading drive was going for the Arabs. Such a drive, we have seen it probably was, that gave irresistible force to the Persian advance under Darius and Cyrus. Certainly some sense that he was carrying Hellenic culture gave point to the energy of Alexander. For a short time the Arabs, too, were irresistible with the simplicity of their idea. It cut through the complexities, elaborations and dubieties of an old and involved civilisation. But after a little while its force of conviction began to fail, and the complexity through which it was cutting began to involve the straight sword itself. And so, still cutting, but less freely and sharply, wound about with the tangle it was reaping down, it suddenly stuck on something as hard as itself. Here was no lush jungle thicket, but a rude stock. If the Arab was hard with desert hardness, here was someone hard as the rocky North. The Arab had started out simple, strong, convinced, loving war, and he had met no one worth his steel, till, out of breath, striking through a curtain of creepers, far from his own ground, he suddenly came on another born fighter, on his own ground, and not less convinced that he too must fight for his most holy faith, as well as for his home. Therefore the Arab was thrown back.

III

So the stage is set for the Middle Ages. The frontiers are drawn that will not shift until the new knowledge begins to stir again in men's minds and another stage of human emergence is opened. Meanwhile, eddying disturbances will rush round the outskirts of Europe as the outlands gradually come under the central influence and the conception of a civilisation which is distinctively European begins to shape itself in the minds of men. These movements are but secondaries, but because they influenced our northern countries and herald our integration into the body of civilisation we must glance at them. Christianity, though in retreat in its homelands of the South and East, is able still to go ahead with apostolic zeal in the North and East. The disappearance of the Roman Empire meant for a moment the disappearance of the Roman Church, but soon it was obvious that the barbarians had been drawn down upon the Empire quite as much by the fascination that a higher culture must have for a more rudimentary, as by the lust weakly riches must rouse in the strong poor. The northern barbarians had reached a psychological condition when action was not enough. We can see by their sagas that they were at this date in a late phase of their Heroic stage. The gods, mighty, fierce, full of action, projections of themselves, still rule, but not only are the Giants always breaking out – that is, not only do men realise that natural forces are really man's master, however lusty he may be – but through these vigorous anthropomorphisms there looms a colder shadow – the shadow of Fate to which men and gods and giants must all bow, before whom the victory of any is as nothing, for whosoever may triumph will but find his shout die in the cold stillness that foretells the heat-death of the Universe. The warm crude anthropomorphism of the Nordic is vanishing, and the hard lines of determinant natural law are showing through. He had no philosophy with which to check the descent into pessimism. Christianity had. It was framed to answer despair and to teach that the declining balance of the worth of this life could and would be adjusted in a world to come. Therefore its success was not in doubt. It came with the prestige of Roman authority, Greek philosophy and Hebrew tenacity to recommend it. Though transcendental enough for any mystic and subtle enough for most philosophers, it was no fantasy, for it claimed and could point to a complete moral evolution – an old and a new dispensation. It had something for every one. From its long scale men could pick that stage of moral stature that suited them; with the additional and very valuable assurance that if they grew in grace there was plenty of room for them to advance and yet be well within the bounds of the new morality. There was not much danger that men would outgrow the Sermon on the Mount. So Christianity spreads into Ireland and up the English coast until Bede records that the Northumbrians, hardly a generation after their conversion, have become so engrossed with their souls, and therefore are hurrying in such numbers into the monasteries, that the land and the army are becoming depleted. This leads to serious consequences. Martel had not only struck back the Mohammedan invasion on the West. He had supported Boniface with military aid, so that the Saxons had double reason for accepting Christianity – it was not only truer, it was stronger than their tree worship. The higher culture that Christianity carried with it, therefore, went forward into the North-east and the barbarism of tribes intensely warlike but completely unorganised could not stand against it. These barbarians had in their favour great courage, a love of war and a knowledge of iron smelting and tempering. Their weakness was a frame of mind – too rudimentary to be called a philosophy – that was, as we have seen, on the brink of despair, and, at the same time, a lack of social organisation and a passion for individual independence that made them politically and even strategically negligible. The hit-back of the Norse invasions on to England and the north coast of Europe in the ninth and tenth centuries was caused by the Scandinavian peoples undergoing the first contractive pressure of social centralisation. Harold Blue Tooth began to build up a single centralised state, and the passionately independent jarls, resenting this political evolution, swarmed away from his control. Their situation and the advance of their technical skill had brought them to the stage when men become capable shipwrights and seamen. The weak state of the lands opposite them gave them an easy objective. They are not sea lords like the Cretans and the Phœnicians. They are only the nomads of the steppe, after a rest in valley farms, moved on by authority and pushed out on to the sea. The union and advance of a North European civilisation, which had seemed a possibility at the beginning of the Carlovingian Dynasty, was now retarded and even reversed. The later Carlovingians were weak and quarrelsome. There was no centre to give a lead. Civilisation was again on the defensive and made a poor hand even of that. Why was this so? The explanation is not to be found in the acts of individual men. The rulers were weak because the situation did not call out strong men, and when one, like the English Alfred, appears, he can only just hold his own – he cannot reverse the process which is going on. If history is the history of man's emergent mind, then we shall be able to discover why this northern civilisation of the ninth and tenth century, after its vigorous beginning, was so soon reduced to the defensive. The explanation seems to be that no civilisation can rise above its source, and the source of this civilisation was not high. Its source was the Christianity of the later Roman Empire. Now Christianity carried the Roman Empire because it agreed with the pessimism of civilised thought. That thought was in despair. It was looking for escape, disillusioned with thought. Christianity won because it preached contempt for this world, confirmed men's suspicion that this life was a failure and promised, if men ceased to question, to try and understand and to struggle, if they believed, accepted authority and renounced this life, its pomps and power, salvation after death. It was this ascetic otherworldly system of thought which won the Empire, and its fruits had to be monasticism and a cult of the dead. As the Empire and this system came to terms each yielded something. The Empire, as we have seen, raised a magician to an equal place with the commander-in-chief. A sort of dual kingship – one for this world and the other for the world to come – was the first concordat. The Church in return allowed the general to carry on, permitted him a share of supplies and granted him levies. It was a weak combination, but even this compromised civilisation seemed a superior thing to the barbarians in the North. Not only were they awestruck by the subtle arguments with which theology established the certainty of the misgivings and fears that had already attacked them, they were also impressed by the remains of the Greek culture and the Roman organisation that the missionaries brought with them. Later, in Russia, the Greek monks were not only to bring to their Muscovite converts letters and a logomachic learning, but also Greek fire and catapults, so that they were helped to sustain their struggle as foothills of civilisation against the levelling flood of the nomad Tartars. So, too, in the earlier centuries the great order of the West, the Benedictine, went north as carrier of a culture higher than the barbarians could themselves achieve. But not much higher, and fatally limited. For not only was the monastic knowledge limited – a third-hand recollection of Greek discoveries – but it was debarred by authority from the spirit of free enquiry. The Church and the Gospel were not based on demonstrable experiment, but on authority, which is the reverse. To question, to ask for proof, to experiment, this was to be lost and excommunicated and damned. And the monastic spirit wished to have it so. The spirit that sought the monastery and found in it its highest expression, was a spirit which called for authority and dreaded exploration. Learning was a side line – the end was salvation. Learning was something with which to keep the mind distracted while the soul worked out its salvation with fear and trembling and waited until Providence saw fit to release it through death into a world attainable without learning and where learning would be useless. It is clear, therefore, that a culture, itself third-hand, circumscribed by an iron authority, and taught by men whose hearts were wholly elsewhere, would be neither advanced nor capable of further advance. This seems the explanation why, though the Norse invasions were checked, and the pagan Hero, Cnut, is turned into a Christian statesman, whose authority extends over the North European littoral and there is nothing further to fear from barbarism, this victory of civilisation does not lead to an advance. One step up has been taken and then progress is arrested. The monasteries held the front, and the monastic outlook was turned away from this world and the avenues of Science more resolutely than was that of the Mohammedan mollahs and muftis. Through these centuries, therefore, we watch the countries of the North and East one by one raised to the level of civilisation at which the Roman Empire went to pieces and there arrested. In some details they are more advanced – the slavery that degraded the Roman Empire and which the otherworldliness of Christianity made it indifferent to combat – was not pleasant to Northerners, and though the failure to understand and control money – where again as we shall see the Church's providentialism was unhelpful – again was to bring about serfdom, it was an economic accident that the serf was 'adscripted to his glebe.' He was personally not an untouchable. In other details the Northern newly Christianised countries were more backward. The legionary organisation, the skill in strategy and fortification were lost. Fighting for the Nord was still a sport in which he was not going to have his individual pleasure spoiled by discipline and professionalism. The idea of being on the defensive – of great camps, lines and walls – was ridiculous to him. The effort would have bored him and, achieved, they would have been useless. As we have seen, he liked to lie over the land in his open farmsteads, and if every now and then fighting came his way all the better. His villages, quite indefensible, straggling for miles, each stead well out of touch with the next, can still be recognised in eastern-lying counties, while the tight ball of the Keltic townlet rolled like a frightened hedgehog, marks the Western people's reaction to a pressure against which they were always on the defensive. Roman Law, also, with its elaborate provision for all the contingencies of city life and the inter-contractive obligation of a society organised to master individualism, this system they heeded even less than the Roman military organisation. Nor was this wholly loss. Roman Law was a machine of marvellous finish, but its liberal use of torture and the whole concept of sanctions and enforcement show that this machine only ran if fed with human suffering.

IV

The civilisation of Europe of the eleventh century is therefore divided into two layers. North lies a level approximating to the level of the Roman Empire at its fall, and evidently unable to rise further. South lies a level a little above this. The Arab power was now in its decadence. The unity of the great Mohammedan belt was broken. Research among Mohammedans had frequently been suppressed and had almost come to a standstill. But still the level here was above the late Roman Empire, and may be taken to be not much below that of the end of Greek culture, about A.D. 100.

So the mind of man remained arrested. The strength of the monastic theologic system was great. Intellectually it was adequately equipped to silence, if not to answer, any rudimentary speculation, and psycho-socially the monastery was perhaps the most perfect machine for stabilising society that has ever been discovered. For the monastery is a guard house into which all individuals who want to explore for themselves and are tired of the settlement of society, can be induced to enter. Here, they are told, is the one gate to the higher life. They enter, the door closes, and whatever happens to them inside, they are dead to the outside world, which continues its way freed of their disturbance. We see the strength of this system, which wielded imponderables, when we watch the struggle in the eleventh century of the Papacy and the German Emperors. These latter had all the physical powers, but the Papacy won, and when Heinrich the IV stood in the snow outside Canossa, waiting for Hildebrand to admit him, the North European civilisation realised that it still stood more in awe of a magician than of a general. If choice of obedience had to be made, the magician could still win. A civilisation so minded is not going to advance. Authority can still cry halt and it will stand. The advance came, therefore, not from the world, but from the Church. The Church had won, but the men who ran it knew how precarious was its power, and they themselves were more surprised by their victory than the conquered soldiers. Hildebrand was actually in retreat when the Emperor sought him out to capitulate. The Churchmen knew the weakness of their magic, for increasingly were they calling on the state to enforce their decrees with physical violence. A Pope of the Dark Ages had instructed the Bulgarians that they must not use torture because it was contrary to the Laws of God and Humanity. This Bishop believed in moral power. But in the dawn of the new enlightenment the Church increasingly calls for violence. Men can no longer be held by magic, and the Church fears to depend on moral prestige. Moral prestige is an immense force. No doubt it, as well as the dread of magic, helped to turn back Attila when, unarmed, Pope Leo went out to face him and saved Rome.

But since then the Pornocracy has intervened. The conduct of the Papacy and the morality of the Popes had shocked the simple, violent but continent 'barbarians.' Moral prestige is an immense force, but it takes an immense effort and no little time to generate it, and a few scandals will dissipate it. So the Church trusts more in force, and, *ipso facto*, has less moral power. The rank and file also were disillusioned. The most distinctive characteristic of pristine Christianity is Apocalypticism – the expectation that the present natural order will at some moment, perhaps quite close, suddenly be exploded and a complete moral order will appear behind it, faced by which, and in its light, every soul will be judged as to his actions in this phenomenal and trial world. This Apocalypticism is a feature that the most searching criticism into Christian origins only seems to establish more authentically. It is, also, the only explanation and justification of the Christian Ethic as found in such early passages as the 'Sermon on the Mount.' This extreme abstentionist morality can only be satisfactorily explained, as Dr. Schweitzer has explained it, as 'an ethic of the interim.' It is a kind of moral holding one's breath. Men are to abstain from everything, and then when they have shown by this intense passive courage that they have perfect faith, then suddenly the mountain will be moved, God will appear, and the new order will be established. And, thirdly, we know that this Apocalyptic standpoint is central in

Christianity because the Church, do what it will, condemn such dreams as often as it may, is never easy in its own mind. At every tremor she starts. 'Was that the footstep of the Judge approaching?' Her policy is therefore always makeshift. She is gagging with her eye on the door. The year 1000 shook, therefore, the faith of Christendom deeply. Chiliasm had helped to make men look upon that year as decisive. It was now or never for the off-deferred, fearful hope. As it approached, leases fell in, and men felt that business was hardly worth while. It came, it passed, and the world went on. Never again would Apocalyptic expectation rise anything like as high. Christianity was weaker. The attention of men went back to business. The world grew more complex. From this, fresh moral problems arose. As we have seen, money came back into its important place. Problems of interest and usury again needed settlement. The Church, conservative, providentialist, tried to deny them altogether. It could not see that money is simply a form of power, of energy rendered preservable and that, therefore, if it is lent, during the time it is out and working for someone else, its owner has a right to be paid. Instead of attempting to adjudge what that due was, the Church could only echo one of Aristotle's least scientific mots: Money is barren, it will not breed if put by, *ergo* any interest is unjust.[1] The Church,

---

[1] It is one of the inevitable tragedies of greatness that its mistakes are usually more honoured than its inspirations.

therefore, was full of misgiving. Fresh moral problems in society, a weakening of faith among the people, and the fact that she herself had increasingly to call on the secular arm to aid her, must have made Churchmen speculate. Events grew worse. The clergy grew slack and despised, and suddenly the worst happened – a counter faith unexpectedly appeared in East Europe, and without arms spread rapidly from Bulgaria to Provence. The Church was panic-struck. Faced with the horror of Catharism – an organised religion that challenged and denied Catholicism – the Church realised she was in extreme danger. This was not moral slackness or witchcraft or sporadic heresy. It was a proof that her magic and organisation might be completely outbid on the open market. It was, therefore, against Catharism that the Inquisition was organised and the Inquisition was a turning - point for the Church and for civilisation. It was the third stage of Christianity. In the first it had been a doctrine of simple otherworldliness. Its appeal to a tired world was its fresh and kindly spirit, a spirit of love which solved all difficulties by saying that if men would only trust, in quite a little while all the cloud of this heavy world would roll away, and the sun of eternity shine down on innocent children for ever. In the second stage it had been a doctrine of subtle authority – to tired civilised and simple barbarian it taught that it held the keys of Heaven and Hell and the civilised saw that it certainly had assurance and energy, and the barbarian saw that it had accomplishments and knowledge greater than his. In the third stage it became definitely an order, a great unlimited liability company armed with a terrible secret service (the Inquisition) and garrisoning the territories over which it had asserted its suzerainty with the monasteries. In this stage the Church will, of necessity, forward learning. She is being attacked. She must gather every force, and unite them all under her banner and for her cause. To understand this, the medieval, phase of civilisation, we must, therefore, watch the development of the Orders.

v

It is not provincial so to concentrate on Catholic Europe. The Moors are already exhausted. Their scientific speculation ended; soon in Spain they were even militarily on the defensive. The Arab civilisation is at a standstill.[1] Soon the Mongol invasions are to begin like avalanches sliding down from the 'roof of the world' on China, on India, on Mesopotamia, on Russia, on Asia Minor. These invasions, the last that the Heroic nomad will make, show him as 'uncivilised' as ever. To the horse he adds the use of

---

[1] Mohammedanism, though a persecuting religion, did not in its decadence organise intelligence and torture to defend it. Because it was a soldier's religion it had always depended on frank force. The ascetic is always subtler and more cruel than the soldier.

artillery. But a simple destroyer he remains, until, after these last raids, civilisation, through science, attains a height of defence which he never again can hope to overrun. At the date, therefore, that we have here reached, Western Europe alone has a clear run of centuries ahead of it for undisturbed internal development.

Monasticism was the distinctive social pattern of successful Christianity. Indeed, we may say, 'No monk, no Catholicism,' is more true than, 'No bishop, no king.' Up to this date the Western Church had been content with Benedictinism as the Eastern Church has never had any order save that of St. Basil. But the quiet classical culture and sane abstinence of Benedict's rule no longer satisfied the ardours of the day. There was occasion for reform. The monastic life is always becoming 'relaxed.' But the real reason for reform, the reason why new rules were organised, was to meet a new peril. The Dominicans are the fathers of the Inquisition. But it is not enough simply to crush bodies. You must answer arguments and build up the minds of the faithful, whose resistance has been undermined. So the great intellectual reorganisation of the day is also undertaken and carried through by a Dominican. The genius of Thomas Aquinas managed to organise the whole of known knowledge. He was not creative. His task was to balance the great mass of Aristotle's knowledge, now again come upon the mental market of the world, with the practical rulings of authority, and to make all these a-moral facts fit in with the cosmology which the Church had projected as sanction of its morality. From Zeno to Aquinas we can trace a single curve of intelligence. With Stoicism, thought dips down below the 'datum line' of free enquiry to the level at which facts are only acceptable and indeed considerable in so far as they support Ethics. The system is everything, and if facts do not support it, so much the worse for the facts. This is the attitude of all medieval thought. It is always aimed at answering rather than accepting facts. With Aquinas we see the last effort so to compass into one rigid, traditional and authoritative system, predominantly utilitarian, moral and rational, all known facts. New knowledge was not wanted, but when unavoidable was adopted. After Aquinas, the system could contain no more. Henceforward the task of civilisation was to make a system and an ethic out of the new natural knowledge. But though not inventive, such a work as the Summa approaches an invention. Though it always ends by finding authority to have been right it has to begin by being ready to accept that this needs proof, and so authority might be wrong. Inevitably, therefore, we find that this attempt is not without its dangers. As there were heroes before Achilles, so, prior to Aquinas, there were keen, devoted, and gifted minds, but in their attempt to reconcile the forces they recognised, they themselves were shattered. As far back as the dawn of the twelfth century, Abelard had wished to defend the Church as much as St. Thomas, but for some reasons his sums did not work out. Perhaps facts, those syrens which the theologian while he sails on the ship of the Church, must dare to listen to, lured him to forget that his task was to guide the ship safely past them. That the mind of man is once again opening to the complexity of the outer world and once again turning outward and taking up its task of facing facts and making sense, is made quite clear by its next step. After the Dominican order came the Franciscan. The Carthusian order is not in the succession. It is of great interest, however, and needs notice. For indeed, it may have contributed to the weakening of the Church, of which it seemed the rarest flower. Rising at the close of the eleventh century, it may actually have drawn away into its silence many enthusiasts who, if they had remained in more 'open' Orders, must have actively strengthened the 'secular' Church. We know that when the storm broke that the Church was accused, and with much show of proof, of hopeless slackness. And the mere fact that such an Order could be founded and actively recruited showed that there was abroad among the best of men a passion to escape and a hatred for the world, which were little short of the Catharist despair.

The real development of the monastic evolution was therefore not Carthusianism but Franciscanism, not to a closer life but to one more in touch with the world. The religious were not to escape but attack. The enthusiasm the new Order awoke was immense, and showed how it responded to a need in men's feelings. It spread rapidly through all the Catholic countries. Preaching was its *raison d'être*. Men were to be won to a life of far-sighted godliness by the eloquence and the arguments of an Order that went up and down among them, understood their tasks and difficulties, and which showed how a life higher than the life of impulse, a life with the longest purpose, could be lived in the dense rush of ordinary living. Thomas Aquinas had written that the Catholic faith was something that could be argued out, it was an intellectual proposition. The Franciscans followed up his writing. Inevitably we see that the interest of men, even on the side of the Church, is shifting from magic and emotion to morality and argument. It is therefore quite natural if surprising to find St. Bernardino of Siena, a Franciscan preacher, saying that a population which grows up without hearing preaching grows up incomparably more irreligious than that which has no Mass. So, too, is it natural that in this Order appears the first experimental scientist of the Modern World. Thomas Aquinas had incorporated Aristotle into theology; now Roger Bacon would incorporate Natural Science. Had not Aquinas said God could be demonstrated? He would observe the outer world and make theology by each observation more firm and wide and impregnable. His order was filled with providentialist qualms, but the Pope, knowing how much the Church needed munitions, and that if she did not move and annex new fields of knowledge others would, specially approved his zeal, and ordered him to pursue his studies.

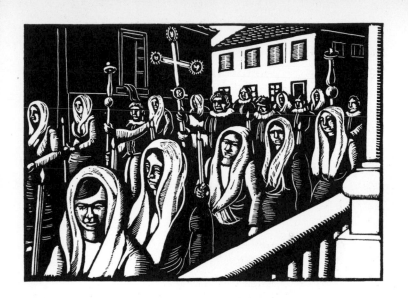

CHAPTER XII

THE AGE OF FAITH BECOMES THE AGE OF HYPOTHESIS

I

THIS resumption of man's mental evolution by the North European branch, is marked by a double advance. This, as we have seen, was characteristic of mental evolution when it was manifesting itself through the Greek and then through the Arab cultures. The advance in observation of the outer world was complemented by an advance in the power of abstraction. Man not only had a new power of noticing things. That by itself must have

253

led to confusion. He had a new and correspondingly enlarged power of ordering these findings, of making them make sense. This dual process, this mental reciprocation, has not been sufficiently realised. In the heyday of Science and Research men have thought that Science is simply observation, and they have marvelled with a certain self-ignorant self-satisfaction that other ages remained so obstinately ignorant, and failed to realise that they only had to look about them to understand and to control. But we now see, in these later years of our scientific phase, that that is a very one-sided way of presenting man's problem. Science is not simply observation, the setting down with exactitude any happening. Consciously or unconsciously science is highly selective. 'Science is measurement' has defined Karl Pearson. How then came it by its Rule? No advance in objective observation could be made until man was equipped with an instrument with which to cut into the continuum, with which he finds himself surrounded, bite off standard pieces and with these artificially limited bits of reality build up an extension of his own human world. It is because of this, because the outer world has really no divisions and so is really immeasurable, that it is true to say that concepts must come before precepts; that we do and can only perceive what we can take in, conceive and make sense of; that, in short, every new advance of knowledge of the outer world must wait upon a new faculty and technique of comprehension. So we see why it is that man's mind has emerged in a series of steps. These steps are only the outward sign of the reciprocating process described above. First there must be what, when it is unconscious, is called a faith, and when conscious an hypothesis.[1] The coming of this faith or hypothesis is perhaps always sudden, unforeseen, revolutionary. It springs from the depth of the mind of which consciousness can have no direct cognisance. The Law of every stimulus, the Law of All or Nothing, seems to rule this, the supreme mental activity, as it does the stimulation of the simplest nerve. For an æon, mind has been stabilised against its conditions. It only admits and recognises certain selected experiences, and to these its reaction grows more and more perfect. So we perceive the common mental principle that underlies such apparently different things as Instinct and a classical Style. In both cases the admission of outer experience has been so limited and constant that finally it can be turned into an adequate appropriate form almost unconsciously. The process of perception and conception is so practised that the practitioner is not only unaware that there could be any other reaction, he is unaware that there is anything else existing other than that to which he reacts. Then, with man, a sense of exhaustion begins to appear. He wearies of his masterly

[1] To-day it is conscious and so men deplore the decline of faith, not realising that never were hypotheses more inspiring and fertile. Faith has to vanish that it may be transferred into its intenser phase, Hypothesis.

finish. He wonders whether there is anything else. The classic period, as it draws to a close, is producing a vacuum. It works up and uses up every scrap of the section of 'raw continuum' which its system, its concept, its hypothesis, its faith, has been able to grasp and accept. Yet there is sound fear holding men back from opening the chamber of the mind in which, like a casson, they are living, and admitting from the unknown no doubt a rush of new air, but air perhaps impossible for them to breathe. Suddenly some mind or minds conceive how a new expansion might be made. They cannot consciously describe their new hypothesis, they only know they have a new power of facing reality, a new faith that they can go forward and grasp with courage, and a sense of value and meaning, a fresh and larger area of reality. They are no longer afraid of the old perfect form being shattered. They welcome variety, lack of scale, even apparent incoherence. This, as we have seen, is the Romantic phase, and this is why it must always alternate with the Classic. There is a crisis. Men are divided into reactionaries and revolutionaries. There is a sudden intense attack of Natural Selection. For as we have seen,[1] Natural Selection has not been stopped by civilisation – rather it has been intensified. But as evolution has with man ceased to be physical, all his changes which have transformed him from a beast to a rational being having been changes in his psyche and not

[1] p. 124.

his physique, so, too, Natural Selection now continues, not physically but psychically. The test for men now, is not whether they can stand changes in their physical, but in their mental climate, in their mental circumstances and the pressure of thought rather than in their bodily environment and the pressure of atmosphere. The inadaptable types go to the wall. The reactionary must fail. That is not to say that he may not check temporarily the new advance. He may persuade the greater part of the society in which he lives not to accept the fact that the old bounds have been swept away. Then, instead of the change disintegrating the mass, and individual by individual the alteration taking place – the mass will remain solid and collapse solid. We see an example of this in our own age. The countries and cultures which denied the hypothesis of the Renaissance, the faith of Humanism, the belief that Science can and must be followed and that only in transcending the narrow anthropomorphism of the former classic period can the spirit of man advance and grow, these countries have not been able to escape Science. Instead of gradually adapting their lives to its methods and outlook they have tried to deny the hypothesis on which it is based and yet to employ such consequences of that hypothesis as proved convenient. In consequence they are completely undermined and unprepared. So Russia fell into the gulf of revolution that must swallow those societies which permit this gap to open between

their acts and their faith. For the same reason
Spain now seems on the brink of a similar fate.

II

This general survey of Faith and Hypothesis helps
us to understand the mental process that lay behind
the dawn of the Renaissance and to recognise,
beneath the local features and topical characteristics,
the resumption of evolution, the further emergence
of man. Man was about to make new discoveries,
Science was about to advance with unparalleled
speed, because man was enlarging his technique of
measurement, his power of more comprehensive
abstractions from raw reality. And this enlargement
of technique, this power of taking a much wider
grasp upon the outer world, of daring to make sense
and order, though in that sense and order his
physical self seemed reduced to insignificance, this
enlargement and power rose from a new faith, a
sudden expansion of mind. There was a conviction,
unconscious but intense, that the Church was wrong,
that the new science, the new cosmology, was not
going to make morality impossible and lead to the
breakdown of civilisation. Such was that expansion,
so long was that step, that the men who took it
may be excused for thinking that they had, at the
one stride, come up against the bounds of reality.
So no doubt assumes the Bee, the undisturbed
Australian Black, the isolated Fundamentalist. The

first late medieval experimenter, the renaissance Humanist and all thinkers of this our phase of mental emergence, right down to the pre-psychical scientist of yesterday, not one could have escaped the conviction that they had touched the bounds, not only of their comprehension, but of their apprehension, and so of reality itself.[1]

The new faith, the faith in the new reason was of course manifested by a new advance in mathematics, and the new advance in mathematics reciprocated with the new advance in 'natural philosophy,' the observation and ordering of the outer world. Such was the world when the Franciscan movement had spent its energy and, as a final spurt, threw up the speculative genius of a Bacon. At this point we may say Europe again won the same height of civilisation which the Roman Empire, applying Greek genius, had attained. The Greek world, immensely creative, had nevertheless been proportionately vulnerable. Thereafter the sites of civilisation were much better guarded from outside interference, and though the shadow of these walls, Macedonian, Ptolemaic, Roman, checked the full growth of the mind, which needs the sun of freedom, nevertheless, though new plants did not sprout, the old ones still bore:—the Academy at Athens where Aristotle and his pupils continued under Macedonian protection – the

---

[1] A few might have made the reservation that behind all that their senses could at present touch, there was further reality, but even it, they would have assumed, was only hidden, not different; an extension of what was experienced, not a completely new quality.

Museum at Alexandra where, as we have seen, the steam engine is being thought about when Egypt had already become a Roman province. The Roman world was hardly creative at all, but many of the Greek ideas were allowed to develop in the Greek preserve of the Empire and, in passing, it may be asked, whether it was not better that the Greek plants should live an overshadowed life with a diminished yield than that, free to sprout and seed, they should also have been free to be cut down altogether. Certainly the Greek colonies, such as the Chersonese, that never fell under the shadow of the Empire, did not show a continued intensity of intellectual life. The intellectual condition of Europe in the thirteenth century is then closely resembling that of the fourth. Both had at their disposal the vision of Plato, the science of Aristotle, the mathematics and geometry of the Museum, the medical knowledge of Galen. Roman Law is almost as widely known in the countries that remained Christian in the thirteenth century as in the fourth century. The monastery is, perhaps, by the thirteenth century, more of a drag than a help to civilisation, owing to the fact that it preserves, but does not originate knowledge, and so tends to pedantry and the active discouragement of research. Money is still a problem, causing almost more trouble than it is worth; and the Church is still proving unhelpful in solving the social complications that must be surmounted if money is to be a convenience and not an embarrassment to civilisation. The national states, however, through their smallness, escape many of the problems of 'book-keeping' which were so serious to the Empire. The improvement in armament is also a very mixed blessing. The heavy armed horseman did, however, make any central power with its knights able to prevail against local uprisings and when, in the century after – the fourteenth – gunpowder came in, this again told in favour of centralised authority. Only a king could cast cannon, and, as grave an achievement, convey with train of ammunition, powder and expert gunners, these immense pieces over the countryside. The authority which was strong enough to forge and wield this weapon, was by that strong enough to beat flat all opposition within its range. The old horror of anarchy of which England tasted, in the distracted reign of Stephen, and the continent knew for generations more, had as its symptom the robber's hold, the impregnable castle. When artillery could 'slight' any tower, the king's train of cannon could drive the path of his authority as straight and make it as irresistible as the cannon shot itself. The trouble was that the kings were seldom content with achieving their peace, but saw it simply as a means for making more trouble for their neighbours. The limits of the national boundaries, which were now setting, seem mainly to have arisen, on the open land, through the limit to which a ruler could rush with his knights in time to put down secessionist revolt or neighbourly invasion. The frontiers of the European nations are in this sense mainly horse frontiers and so, incidentally, frontiers which, with every increase in speed of transport, become more ludicrously petty. Beyond the riding limit another state could grow up, whose size also was similarly limited by the fact that up to a certain point it could successfully repel invasion and beyond that point it could itself less and less successfully invade or at least annex. In consequence, this energetic Europe, possessed of most of the faculties of the Roman Empire, few of its obligations, and much more than its spirit – indeed with a passionate vitality that had exterminated such defeatists as the Cathari – was not over-strong, and when the peril of the barbarian invasions again loomed, it was luck and not united management that saved Europe. Had the Tartar invasion started from a base less remote than Kara Koram – a base so distant that to these raiders China was really the obvious prize and not a few quaint little nations living on the world's edge by the final ocean and the setting sun – then instead of only Russia becoming their slave all Europe might. As it was they may actually have helped Europe by making it impossible for a rising Russia to resume on the part of Byzantium the quarrel of the Eastern and Western Empire. While there can be no doubt Timour's defeat of the Sultan Bajazet, when he was on the verge of taking Constantinople, preserved that centre, until

Western Europe could benefit better by the seed which was scattered when this ancient tree finally fell.

The fall of the Eastern Roman Empire is then the beginning of the Modern Age, because, though it meant that a barbarian – a Muslim who would never have the Arabs' unorthodox taste for science – was in Europe and would come as far west as Vienna, the rising flame of understanding would not be chilled by this presence, but, swept into a focus, would burn the more briskly. Greek scholars, wrenched up, came into an Italy which honoured and stimulated them and was stimulated by them. A narrow line of universities from Sicily to the English Midlands poured together all the knowledge they could find and fermented the whole. There were bound to be explosions. Men were questioning everything, and wanting to experiment with everything. The Church was nervous. No doubt the presence of the Turk at the door did not make her more inclined to be liberal. In the French Revolution, it has been noted, the intensity of the Terror always indicates how near the invaders are to Paris. So when the growing medical faculty wanted to dissect dead human bodies, the Church would not give leave. When astronomy, having again reached the point where Ptolemy stopped, wished to go on to a larger hypothesis, again the Church vetoed. Copernicus, being a bishop, understands the need of caution and dies unprosecuted, leaving his bombshell of a book to explode in publication after he had gone. Galileo, not a Churchman, but only a scientist, and an irritable one at that, gets his fingers caught in the cruel machine, as too carelessly he is brushing aside medieval lumber. And Bruno, who was positively rowdy, whose spirit is really not scientific but rather that of an inverted theologian, actually provokes the Church to put itself completely in the wrong by burning one who was maintaining, whatever his motive, a scientific fact. And to these blunders of doctrinaire cruelty the Church added a greater blunder of inconsistent indulgence. The awaking world might endure a Church that was indulgent, even expensive, if humane. It might also have stood – part of it has stood since – a Church that was intolerant, even cruel, if sincere. But the mixture of vices and the absence of virtues was too much and North Europe broke away. This was a set-back for the human mind. There can be little doubt it would have been better for civilisation if the Rennaissance had not ended in the Reformation, but that uninterrupted Humanism had continued, with perhaps the northern speculation always somewhat circumscribed, but certainly with the southern speculation continued. The Church's dogmatic system would then not have been broken, part discarded and part more rigidly imposed, but it might have been gradually stretched completely out of shape and until it could admit all the new knowledge. The sum of knowledge, say by

1830, would then one may assume, have been rather greater than it actually was.

Yet when we make such a remark, we need to remind ourselves that we are thinking, as till lately we could not help ourselves, as though the advance of knowledge was not only an unmixed good but worth any price of social dislocation. Indeed, we have had no patience with men for being so old-fashioned as to be upset by new facts that leave their old morality baseless. Yet, we now ought to realise that such an attitude on our part is pre-psychological. The strength of a chain depends on every one of its links. And though, even in the Renaissance, and increasingly to-day, there are many men at the top who have the vitality and vision to push on and to believe that an ever greater morality will develop from an ever greater knowledge of the outer world, that is not so of the rank and file. The other links that hold these farthest and latest forged rings of the chain of social life, and keep them supplied and in touch with ordinary living, these links were not then, and are not yet, ready or able to give as elastically as the men at the top would like. The society in which a philosopher lives (as we have seen when watching the dawn of science in Ionia) is really as important as the philosopher himself, as the oyster is as important as the pearl. So the thinker must be just as much dependent on, and a consequence of his society as is a baker or a butcher. Society produces what it needs. If it turns vegetarian, butchers must face unemployment. If it feels that science is going too fast for its morality to adapt, scientists must not be surprised if it checks their activity. The light-footed child may run ahead skipping over chasms. But the ponderous mass of society, like a burdened elephant bringing up the rear, must try each plank to see whether it will stand its tremendous weight.

So history went the way it did probably because, beside the taste for new knowledge, the need of carrying on actual living without a breakdown, has also constantly to be met.

III

The secession of Northern Europe meant then that the Church had to set her house in order. If she was to counter attack, if, even, she was to save herself from attack on her very base, she must undergo military training. Indulgency must be banished. The Church became consistent, ascetic, increasingly intolerant. The North also flamed with militant conviction. Here was no atmosphere of growing understanding. Yet the evolution of know-ledge was not stopped in the northern lands. Kepler refuses to become a Catholic because it would mean that his astronomical advances would be checked. He is a devout man, but his devotion incorporates with it devotion to Truth. In other words, he has the vitality which can go on because, contrary to

Catholic authority, it can believe that everything it discovers must somehow have worth to the human spirit, and nothing can be found that will degrade it. And even more remarkable and hopeful, even the Church could not avoid trying to use the keys, which had opened a new world for man, to lock him up again. We have seen that the great religious Orders are each of them with their great temporary enthusiasm and their peculiar character, significant of the mental development of mankind during the Middle Ages. If we had no history of Europe but the history of the Orders we could diagnose its mental development by their evolution. The appearance of the Jesuits would of course prove that a revolution had taken place. This is the answer of the Church to the new frame of mind. Man has emerged until what was implicit in his actions has become explicit in his mind; his faith has condensed into hypothesis. And yet as we have seen, that condensation was really an expansion. It is true he became more conscious of how he went about to find things out. But also at the same time, in his unconscious, he made another vast step forward. 'He accepted the Universe,' he accepted Truth, he accepted a new technique of discovery on the hypothesis or in the faith that, if he pressed on with it, it would not betray his trust, that he was serving something greater than himself, and that in that service he was in some way, and as he could not be otherwise, fulfilled. 'Yea, though it slay him yet

would he trust in it.' The Church realised that such
an attitude was of immense strength. Through this
daring vision though man lost his soul, undoubtedly
he did find unparalleled power. So reason should
not be slighted. As we have seen, first the Church
had advanced because of a bright contempt for the
world: that was its triumph over the Roman society.
Then it had advanced because it knew the wisdom
of this world and the mystery of the world to come:
that gave it victory over the barbarian tribes. Then,
as men settled down and learnt to argue, increasingly
the Church has to argue. Moral prestige is much,
the power to work miracles is more, but holiness and
miracles neither appear over easy to command. The
supplies are never equal to the need. The call upon
the secular arm and the organisation of the Inquisition may have seemed unavoidable owing to the
unsatisfactory yield of saints and thaumaturgists,
but so to supplement poor spiritual powers is to
assure their further failure. So when the secular
arm became indifferent or even hostile, the Church
had to take to argument. The Dominicans and the
Franciscans had marked the beginning of the
preaching campaign, but it was largely exhortation,
propaganda. After the Reformation, the Church
had really to argue; and to argue with an informed
adversary you must have knowledge. You cannot
leave him to get up the facts and then meet him as
an equal in debate. Therefore, the Jesuits are to
know all that is to be known and constantly to find

and to show that it agrees with and confirms what the Church has already decided. This is to ask of men a super-human service. Thomas Aquinas was a genius, but he only had to reconcile the theology of his day with Aristotle. The Jesuits are called upon to keep on reconciling constantly expanding knowledge with a rigid system. The Counter Reformation nevertheless for a short time seemed to promise the restoration of the Church. The counter attack began to carry the lost positions. The Protestants were disorganised, negative, without a philosophy and with waning enthusiasm. The right of private judgment was being abandoned for the authority of the Bible, and when the decision had to be between the authority of a living body of men, however self-seeking, and the authority of a collection of books reflecting the varying morality of some thousand years or more, it is not surprising that men, who were faced with the choice and free to take it, often went back to Rome. Nevertheless, the Church could not stop research, and as long as that could not be stopped, as long as North Europe believed, in whatever church it attended, that it was right and not wrong to keep on trying to understand and to discover, so long the wider hypothesis, which makes the modern world, has not been yielded, and the Church's position is outflanked and undercut. The Church, therefore, has been and must be increasingly on the defensive, an organisation that claims toleration because it deals with souls and so may ask the right to comfort individuals and to serve private feelings. It is no longer an authority on the nature of the physical world. The real attempts in the modern world to contain and master the new mind of man have, therefore, not been made by the religious, but by the revolutionaries. The Jesuit rank and file gave the world a display of intelligent devotion that awoke the admiration of all onlookers. The Jesuit leaders gave a display of subtlety and power that awoke something little short of panic in their opponents. But after a couple of generations the opponents were steadily gaining in numbers and in force, and the onlookers knew that the Order had failed. Catholic country after Catholic country made the Pope withdraw these agents until the strange sight was seen of an Order which had been formed to advance Ultramontanism actually disbanded by the Pope and taking shelter with a Protestant King.[1] The Order is re-established by the Papacy, but the virtue has gone from it and now like the Dominicans and the Franciscans it is no longer the channel of a fresh enthusiasm but part of an establishment. It approaches the quiet professionalism of the Lutheran or the Anglican clergy. It no longer challenges or can attempt to control and check the emergent mind of man as that mind advances to the limit of its present hypothesis.

[1] Frederick of Prussia.

CHAPTER XIII

THE SOCIAL REACTIONS

I

YET as soon as it was certain that religion had failed with the Counter Reformation to reimpose its anthropocentric limit, another force appeared, anxious to attempt to restrict the full expansion of man's mind and to make it stop short of its intellectual limits. That force was the Social Revolution. Such an effort was inevitable and, in a way, right. It was really part of the never-ceasing attempt to make human society consistent, to make its faith the explanation of its conduct, and its conduct a complete rendering of its belief. There is and must always be this interrelation and balance of these two sides of man. His cosmology – his concept of the universe as a whole, his scientific outlook, the sum of his perceptions of the outer world – must be that which gives rise to his ethic – his deliberate conduct of his life. And his social behaviour and his ethic – his reaction of living – must be what gives meaning to his outlook. If he cannot live in the face of certain facts either then he will never notice them (they will take toll of his life, no doubt, but he will endure better through denying them than he could endure accepting them as facts, and yet unable in any wise to reconcile them as values) or he will forget that he has noticed them.[1]

The Reformation was, therefore, not merely an

[1] Two things should perhaps be made quite clear here. 'Value' is simple that the fact seems true, interesting, relevant to some series of observations. It does not mean that it supports any conscious theory, though probably it must not conflict too flagrantly with the essential convictions of the day. Its real value is that it is still within the range and compass of the new faith and that faith is, we have seen, unconscious – no one can say where its bounds lie, but they can feel when these have been transgressed. 'Cosmology' and 'ethic' are, at base, unconscious things, and though they seem both objective and only related to each other through conscious adjustment by the human will, they are really two divergent emergent points of a single reaction to life. Men can only, as a mass, perceive such things about the outer world as make social life possible or do not render it impossible. Individuals may see more than is wise. They are scouts put forward, or rather experimental units pushed out to see how they stand the unfamiliar pressure. So society unconsciously can 'try it on the dog.' So a natural selection is again seen working, and those pioneers who survive become the natural leaders of the next age.

arrest of the Renaissance. The Reformation has a positive side. From that side it can be seen as the first Revolution: the first social consequence of the new knowledge, the first attempt, after the elder form (represented by the Church) had broken up, to frame, in its place, another social system to react to and to contain science. The Reformation was unconsciously and crudely an attempt to see how much of the new knowledge could be accepted by being made a practical part of men's actual living, by being incorporated in the 'sanctional' side of morality. The Church, with the Jesuits, thought that all knowledge must be pressed into the earlier anthropomorphic mould – because the Church believed its morality depended for its sanctions on an anthropomorphic cosmology. All knowledge that told against such an interpretation, and could not be made at least neutral, must be suppressed. The Reformation began by being braver than that. Because it had to win its way against a hostile authority, it rallied to its support all who would attack the old inadequate tyranny and the cry with which it united its heterogeneous forces was the 'Right of Private Judgment.' It was the proclamation of the Individual, and it was the claim on his behalf, now that he had come of age, to save or lose his soul by himself. As we have seen that Right would be withdrawn as soon as the Roman power was in retreat. Authority would be reimposed and an authority more of an anachronism than the

Church's. But the Protestant system was never made consistent and water-tight. It was a protest against an anchylosed system. It was a protest in the name of liberty, and so it never could have either the virtues or vices of complete systematisation. It claimed, therefore, to be a sloughing off of unauthorised accretions. Its conscious aim was to restore the flexible spiritual life that the Reformers agreed to find in Primitive Christianity. Why, therefore, was there need to interfere with speculation? It was not necessary to salvation, but neither did it endanger salvation. Science was simply irrelevant to salvation. The Catholic belief that nothing in the universe can be neutral, it must help or hinder religion: the Catholic intelligence that traced the bearing and relation of each outward fact on the inner life: neither of these were acceptable to Protestantism. A man was saved by a simple act of faith. Thereafter, he was free to interest himself in the world as much as he liked, and, as he had far fewer religious exercises, disciplines, rites and services to take up his time, he might as well fill up the days with innocent speculation and research. It has often been pointed out that the business activity and commercial accumulation of the Protestant countries rose largely from the free time and energy left to its practitioners by the simpler religion. It is also true that the scientific advance may be largely attributed to the same occasion.

Protestantism does, therefore, accept more of the

274

scientific hypothesis, permits a further advance of man's mind toward the supra-anthropomorphic faith, than does Catholicism. We see that it possesses a renewed assurance that the universe is not un-friendly, by the fact that the monasteries are abolished. This act is not merely due to kingly greed. Where the carcase was, there were the royal eagles gathered together. The monasteries had long been obviously under-manned. The best men were no longer in despair, the most scholarly no longer needed such protection. The best felt that action was not vain and that they ought to be out in the world. The scholarly also felt that the monastery was not a quiet close but a cramp. The minds that would have been bound in the cloister now were free to sprout in the wind-swept, but sunny open.

The Reformation, therefore, is the first attempt to see, clumsily, piecemeal, unconsciously, how much of the new faith can be incorporated in actual living, and how much actual living dare be enlarged, without rupture, so as to keep in touch with and be based upon the new and far deeper foundations. Protestantism is an effort on the part of northern man to feel his way down to new sanctions and to transfer the bases of morality from the old anthropomorphic cosmology, if not to this new cosmology in which man certainly seemed insignifi-cant, then to a purely sociological foundation. The Reformation fails. The authorities of the North, who call themselves Protestants, are as frightened at the general loosening of morality as are the Catholic authorities. Luther, who had headed the revolt, lives to hound on the princes to butcher the wretched peasants, who thought a new world had dawned. But though the Protestant rulers will not permit men to deduce new morality from the new cosmology, and to assert freedom from the old morals because science has cut away the sanctions on which authority has asserted the old morals depended, these rulers are not consistent. They permit the pursuit of new knowledge, the establishment of the new cosmology, to be continued. So, while maintaining that the house must not be rebuilt, they permit the excavations in its foundations, which have already made it settle, to be pushed forward. In consequence the settlement continues of itself, and in spite of all edicts. Finally, after another couple of hundred years, little more than a shell is left of the old Order.

II

By 1750, Northern European society is much in the same state (of action and belief being at total variance from official statement and outward appearance) as was the Renaissance Church just before the Reformation broke out. Science was still pushing down below all the foundations, practically unchecked. Every one accepted the new Order, but every one who controlled postponed the enormous task of readjustment. Each felt, however certain was the final settlement, the inertia of the mass might just last his time. Because, therefore, the men, who knew the profundity of the change, dreaded undertaking a task which must be precarious and also provisional – for the explorers had not yet touched bottom – reform passed – as seems unavoidable at this stage – into the hands of emotionalists. The first, the religious reformation, had been actually put through not by humanists and scientists but by men who had an emotional and largely un-historical vision of a perfect past. This second, the political revolution, also was put through by emotionalists, who imagined they were reforming society into an even more perfect, more distant, and more visionary past. The Protestants looked back to Primitive Christianity of which they could know little. The revolutionaries for the Rights of Man looked back to primitive society, of which they could know nothing. But where provisional knowledge feared to tread, on these cracking floors of society, from under which Science had already removed nearly everything, the emotional enthusiast rushed in. 'Here,' he cried, stamping his foot, 'All these absurd partitions and crumbling buttresses must go. It is their weight that is making the house crack.' The slum-palace fell like a pack of cards, but it revealed no firm, broad foundation on which a new, commodious workhouse could be built: only an immense excavation down in the dark of which could be heard still the constant blows of the scientific pick. The Revolutionaries reacted as the Reformers before them. The clumsy frame made by aristocrats had been cleared. Now the new must be built. There must be an end of all this tunnelling. The tyrants had been undermined and overthrown. The engineers had served their purpose. It was time to close down the pit. Men must not explore regardless of consequences, but only far enough to set society free to reframe itself on a system of general justice for all. So the Revolution really spoke when its representative said it had no need of chemists. It did not need to know any more irrelevant, unsettling facts about the nature of the universe. It wanted to close down knowledge, sum up science and make a complete, closed, stable system which had come to terms with the universe, and which could carry on without continually having to pay attention to it, and to adapt and alter morals to new findings.

The Political Revolution has, therefore, to go through a stage of vigorous repressing of 'immorality', and Robespierre sends quite as gladly 'anarchists,' immoralists, and Communists to the knife as he sends aristocrats. Indeed this seems an inevitable stage of all revolutions. Onlookers have sometimes wondered why causes that begin by preaching liberty should have to end by being, not only more repressive to critics, but more straitlaced and puritan in themselves than the old authority they overthrew.

The explanation seems to be that the real motive that underlies their action is not love of liberty or understanding (that belongs to scientists who are the symptom of revolutions, but not the leaders of them) but an overmastering desire to make an order more efficient than the old. Revolutionaries are never interested in understanding, but in imposing. They see new knowledge has made the old social reaction (they do not realise that it was once natural and right, and that their solution will one day be as wrong) completely vain and harmful. Their resolve is to make a new system which, by accepting a sufficiency of new facts found out about the world, will endure, for ever holding man in an indestructible organism. When the organism seems to have attained that degree of strength and validity, when it has come sufficiently to terms with the findings of natural science so that it can claim to have some sanction in the outer world, then they wish to close down, stop speculation and experiment, and live settled ever after. Yet each time that the settlement is made a higher proportion of natural knowledge is found in the amalgam -- proportionately less ungrounded moral assumptions. Whoever wishes to estimate this has only to compare, say, the Westminster Confession with the Code Napoleon.

Yet in spite of all attempts to come to terms with it, Science could not be persuaded to stop, or (to put it less anthropomorphically) no social settlement, no morality, was as yet sufficiently enlarged and extended to tally with the facts which the mind of man had been able, and was still able, to find out about the world. The one side of his nature, the social reaction, the 'applied,' the practical side, was still lagging behind the other side, the independent, pure, experimental, speculative side. There was no danger in his going on – quite the reverse. The fact that he could still find out more, was, we have seen, good proof that he could assimilate such knowledge without disaster and that, if he was to have any rest, his social system must become conformable with it. But Natural Selection cannot be removed from our lives. All must undergo the strain of readaptation, and those who dread change must resist it and must die.

III

The end of this sketch is now in sight. All through the nineteenth century, man pushed on with his Science. Unflinching he continued to pierce on every side through the elder anthropomorphic cosmology and to penetrate down, seeking for the limit of his thought. No doubt, as they pressed on, even the most enterprising had misgivings. Even Huxley could turn emotional, as to an Oxford audience he expatiated on the gulf that he and his fellow workers were always widening between what they and he took to be the only possible basis of morals and the only possible conclusions of observation. No doubt he believed himself quite sincere in his regrets, even as Winwood Read saw no inconsistency when, having written of the whole history of man as a martyrdom, he hailed and took farewell of man, freed from the infliction of this martyrdom, as one to be commiserated with because he had had to abandon a delightful dream. However, it is hardly fair first to denounce the past as one long imprisonment and then to complain that the present is spoilt by acute agoraphobia. As a matter of fact, none of these romantics were really unhappy – they were only being quite human and wanting both to eat their cake and have it – both to see things with complete detachment and also to see themselves in the centre of the picture. There was a great deal of Romance and emotional thrill to be got by men, whose lives were more respectable and secure and routined than lives had ever been before, out of the vision of themselves as abandoned explorers drifting on a floe into the night. Read actually sought adventure, but Huxley found relief in the exercise of a fine threnodic style.[1] Their distress was in fact, more what they felt they ought to feel than what they actually felt. We know for certain that they were really not within any measurable distance of despair because they continued, with unabated confidence, energy and fruitfulness, to push on with

[1] Huxley's gloom may have been due, not to a sense of Science's failure to sanction any morality, but due to an unconscious feeling that it was about to sanction *another* morality for which, no more than Bishop Wilberforce, was he prepared.

their upsetting discoveries. The facts continued turning up and filling out their majestic hypothesis, and as they pieced out that design with find after find, though 'with sobs and tears they sorted out those of the largest kind,' it is hard to believe that in their subconscious they were not really jubilant and full of excited hope. It is true they could not say what the goal might be, but they felt they were at last on a strong scent, they were clue by clue pushing into the heart of an immense mystery, elucidating the supreme riddle of the world, and as long as men so think, they are happy. To be unable to put down a good detective story one does not need to know the end – quite the reverse.

So we see nineteenth century Science went unfalteringly on because it was certain that it was making more and more sense, bringing an ever larger number of old facts and new into a single comprehensive system. It might not be apparent where man came in, but a moment's reflection showed that he had a place because he it was who organised the knowledge; it was through the focus of his mind that it took shape. That seemed poor comfort and thin, metaphysical stuff to the simple materialists, religious[1] and scientific, who thought of mind as impossible of being without a body. They were so taken in by the body, and took it so gratuitously for granted, that they never questioned

[1] The religious who believe, as the service of baptism for those of 'riper years' commits them, to resurrection of the *flesh*, are materialists.

that through it they had full objective knowledge of
the outer universe. As they were never tired of saying, they could not doubt the evidence of their senses.
In consequence they could not realise how much
everything they could perceive depended on their
power of being able to accept it, able to make some
sense of it. Had they realised this subjectivity in
their powers they would not have had so much misgiving about using them to the full. For they would
have realised that whatever they perceived, they
perceived it because it had significance for them.
True, it might have no significance for what they
had been. It might, and probably would, make
nonsense of all that had responded to, sanctioned,
and confirmed their old way of living and being.
But it had significance for what they actually were
at that moment, and were in process of becoming.
The new finds in the outer physical world, that
suddenly seemed to reveal a super-human cosmology,
were really indicative of a new expansion in the
inner world of the psyche. This expansion required
to be complemented by a correspondingly vast outer
world. The post-anthropomorphic outlook, the
universe that has no place for little individual lonely
man is, then, not a sudden, unprepared, unaccept-
able but inescapable fact, which at a blow puts out
mind from the cosmos. On the contrary, it is more
than prepared for: it is a consequence of man's mind
having transcended the arbitrary limitations of
individuality. When man emerged on that discovery

he had reached a turning point in his career, a turning point as decisive and far more dramatic than that dim moment when he ceased to be an ape. These are the two great crises of our racial destiny. The first was when man ceased to be an animal, and the second when he ceased to be an individual. In both cases he was probably for a long time (like the new-born) not at all clearly alive to what had befallen him. In both cases many units remained still in the lower state – only a few achieved the higher condition. But in both cases – one millions of years ago – the other in our own day – the transition has been achieved.

But before we can trace the final steps of this emergence and take leave of our story, leaving the amazing being, his wings unfurled from his cocoon and spreading for flight, we must glance at the last and, one dare hope, the final effort to stabilise and to seal him down. We have seen, as his mind in this modern age has advanced rapidly in span and range, how successive efforts have been made to contain it and to make every one of his daring flights to return back to the social ark with the assurance that there is nothing outside it. As these flights have grown ever wider the ark has been enlarged a little, so that realighting might not become impossible. The Religious Reformation was one enlargement. The Political was a second and a much more extensive one. But, in proportion to the increase of knowledge (the much larger area opened up for flight outside the ark) the Political Revolution was probably not as adequate to meet the expanding needs of men as had been the Reformation adjust-ment. Certainly we can see that as a settlement it did not last nearly as long. The Reformation made a stabilisation which lasted some two hundred years – from the last quarter of the sixteenth to the last quarter of the eighteenth century. The stabilisation resulting from the Political Revolution has lasted about a century and a quarter. Now we have reached the third contractive crisis – the third and perhaps the most drastic and determined effort made by the practical, unintellectual social side of man to settle accounts with the expansive spirit – the attack of utilitarianism, upon knowledge pur-sued for its own sake and regardless of consequences. The settlement of the Political Revolution, expressed perhaps most definitely in the Code Napoleon, had accepted much of the findings of Science; the morality it implied was a morality very largely based on the cosmology revealed by Science up to the close of the eighteenth century.[1] But, as we have seen, in spite of that, Science went on enlarging the cosmology, even more rapidly during the succeeding century. This meant that the political settlement increasingly lost prestige. People felt it was unreal. They might have endured its practical insufficiencies

[1] It accepted man and society as both provisional and attempted to adjust them to each other on the empirical basis that the state should not deny to the man any expression which did not endanger it.

and harshnesses if they had felt that it was after all 'true,' if they were persuaded, as its founders probably were, that it did reflect in moral and social terms the nature of the universe. But this the constant accelerating advances of Science made it increasingly difficult to maintain. In consequence, men, who were, either from their sense of wrongs or their love of rights, predominantly concerned with the structure and not with the foundations of society, began to frame a new system to supersede the political settlement. Such an attempt had to be largely the work of sentimentalists and not scientists. This is not to say that these sentimentalists were incapable of careful and thorough deduction. It is to maintain that they were sentimentalists because they were not going to examine their premises. Their motive was an overmastering desire to make a case for their settlement, both against the past settlement and the future uncertainties. So they were alien and hostile to the scientific spirit, which is determined to know all that can be known, and not to conclude until all this knowledge has been ordered, valued, and balanced. So as was the case in the last two great settlements – the Religious and the Political – this third settlement also is the work, not of the new knowledge which has made it necessary, but of emotional man, reacting violently to that new knowledge, and convinced that it can be settled with, once and for all, by imposing on it their new social framework.

IV

This, then, seems the real nature of Socialism and its logical conclusion, Communism. And as the Code Napoleon is the most concrete expression of the Political Revolution Settlement, so Bolshevism is the most definite expression of the Economic Revolution Settlement.[1] In the practice of Bolshevism we can see the same effort being repeated at a later stage. The Soviet accepts more Science than any other state openly accepts and incorporates in its constitution and laws. In this way it is undoubtedly a social settlement, a coming to terms with the new cosmology, a bringing of the state up-to-date, in advance of any other. But its aim is even more limited than theirs. Its goal – because the more definite therefore the more rigid and circumscribed – is not the expansion of mind, the advance of Science and the exploration, to the limit of thought, of the bounds of the new cosmology. On the contrary, its aim is a settlement. Its desire is to shut down on this boundless liberty, this advance without known term of reference. Science and understanding are

[1] It would seem more natural to say Marxism or *Das Kapital*. Here is a complete social-reaction interpretation of the nineteenth-century science. We have the Determinism of physical science made a dogma of human history. But Marx wrote too long before his doctrines were put into practice. In consequence Bolshevism is showing in actual practice as little likeness to abstract Communism as did the Christian Church of the second century show to the teaching of the 'Sermon on the Mount.' Both practices show descent from their original morality but circumstances have modified them so that their points of change are even more striking than their points of agreement.

287

not the ends of the state but its means, its slaves to make firm and for ever its iron system of an immortal unchanging state. The hope of Bolshevism is by using science in every way to have such powers that it will be able to defeat all the societies of the elder model who incorporate and exploit less Science, and also be able to crush every individual within its realm who either still would restore the narrower, elder, superseded model or would – equally treasonable – by action or thought, by indifference or criticism, suggest that the Bolshevik settlement is not final.[1]

V

How long this third settlement can last is the supreme political and social problem of our day. Will it spread as spread the Reformation and the Political Revolution until, not the state, but the idea becomes internationalised – a world phenomenon? There seems to be reason to suppose that this may happen. But how long then will it last? We have seen that the Political Revolution Settlement only lasted about half the time that the Religious Revolution Settlement lasted. Science undermined it. And certainly Science to-day is not only increasing faster than ever; its speed of advance

---

[1] It may be said that the Soviet claims that it advances Science purely for the sake of Science, but let Science, for example, find that 'Proletarian stock' is less good than other stock, and Science would be silenced.

is being accelerated at such a pace that a decade now is equal to a generation a hundred years ago, and certainly equal to a century's advance at the beginning of the Modern Age. Science will undermine the Soviets. The Catholic Church is stronger. Though she touches Science she only does so through the insulator of the Jesuits – an order trained with great psychological insight to be as immune, as far as any human mind may be, to the open influence of argument and to the viewing of facts regardless of consequences. Bolshevism, with its obsession with Economics, despises Psychology. It permits minds, only fortified by rather crude dogmas, to study Science with perilous thoroughness. This is so dangerous to the system because, though applied science can strengthen the material side of the state, pure science must dissolve the idea on which the state is founded. And it is not possible to have a fruitful applied science unless it is based, and amply based, on a pure science. The history of research has illustrated this fact over and again. Only exploration without term of reference allows Science to advance. Here is a paradox as striking as the hedonistic paradox: he who pursues only power will not get it, but he who pursues truth will have power given as a by-product. But if the Soviet power permits pure research it is permitting the exercise of a spirit which is hostile to and corrosive of its dogma. And sooner or later not only will that spirit, by implication, show that the dogma has no objective foundation, it will actually demonstrate that it is contrary to objective fact. So it is not surprising already to find an ever-growing tale of professors prosecuted, not for political activity, but for failing to declare that Science supports, confirms, and is only and wholly manifested and fulfilled in the Soviet State, the Economic Revolutionary Settlement. For Science is not a technique but a spirit, a philosophy, a certain vast expansion of the mind of man. No one can set its limits. We shall only know we have touched them when research becomes barren and exploration fails. That certainly is not to-day nor in sight. However wide, therefore, the Economic Revolutionary Settlement spreads, and however long it lasts, it cannot be final, for not only has it already the seeds of its dissolution in itself, they have already germinated and we can watch them sprout.[1] Were the advances of Science

[1] It may be said that Bolshevism teaches the doctrine of Beyond the Individual, and that therefore it belongs to the future and is not an attempt to prevent man's evolution. It does, however, interfere with the free expansion of man's mind, and as that is the only way in which man can evolve and be led out of his present limiting individuality, it is defeating itself, if its aim is really to transcend individuality. It may have got rid of the competitive element which springs from money (though the reintroduction of piecework seems to contradict this and is undoubtedly a flagrant departure from the principles of Communism), but it is left with the lust for power, and the struggles within the Party show that this Will to Power is sharpening individuality as keenly as does the pursuit of wealth. Indeed the constant interference with the free speculative power of man (which is leading man eventually to transcend his individuality and realise he is only valid as part of a general mind) is such that it appears that in old 'capitalist' countries men are actually advancing more quickly toward real Communism (not a political state so-called, but a state of mind) where men understand clearly that they are parts of an organic whole – than in the

but partial, if the method only applied to physics, then perhaps the Soviet might postpone, if it could not arrest, the oncoming day of settlement. The Church, as we have seen, has attempted to stabilise its front on this line, abandoning physics to Science and hoping thereby to arrive at an agreement that psychology shall still be its province and excepted from the scientific range. But the Church is carrying out this manœuvre with the most highly trained troops – the Jesuits are not only all disciplined to resist argument, they are, many of them, fully learned in the most modern psychology – and even about the Church's partial success there is the gravest doubt. But Science has not only taken all experience as its province; lately it has made advances in psychology which, not only are as profound as any of its advances along all its other branches, but advances which, because of the nature of this particular branch and subject, must have even profounder effects on man than all his other discoveries. It is often lamented, when men to-day survey the emergence of man, and, chief symptom of that emergence, the growth of Science, what a tragedy it was that men's morals did not keep pace with their powers or, in other words, what a pity it was the physics and indeed all other branches of

official Communist country. The truth seems to be that without liberty, Communism cannot grow, any more than Science can grow, because they are two aspects of the same growth of man's mind. Without liberty you do not get Communism but its contradiction, Dictatorship.

Science had to develop before psychology. Yet a moment's reflection shows that it could not have been otherwise. Of necessity man had to come last to himself. He had to gain objective vision first of the farthest things and learn to focus accurately, with a clear and detached sense of the object's real nature and position, on an object with which he was not closely connected. Step by step he has been led to apply the same 'binocular vision' to objects nearer and more intimate. Now at last he can so consider himself. This, as has been said above, is the most revolutionary step which man has ever taken. For at the same time that he learns to be able to watch himself with detachment, he transcends his limitation (which seemed insuperable) not only as an animal but as an individual. He can see how so much of his past thinking was rationalisation, and that even perceptions, which he took to be complete and objective, were so selective as to be quite unreliable. In fact, he can now see not only the picture of the world, but in the picture, himself looking at it. He can not only see how partial and distorted that onlooker's impression must be, but he can take that impression and, through his knowledge of the seer, interpret with an objectivity never imaginable before, the Seen, the world, if not as it actually is, reality *sub specie aeternitatis*, at least as supra-personal mind may see it.

Before, in a final page, we conclude with a speculation as to what further emergence may, in consequence, lie before man, it is necessary in a few words to show why this degree of knowledge, even if it did not point to further degrees, must be fatal to the latest Revolution Settlement. We have seen that while the scientist continued to follow Science, realising that it had not yet summed up, feeling intuitively that it had not exhausted its hypothesis, the social reconstructor, the man who was concerned to make society stabilise on a base satisfactory to his sense of justice, seized upon that stage of scientific advance which seemed the stage which would give the least possible support to the old order and yet not be so extreme as to give no foundation for the new order he intended to impose in place of the old. So Marx talks much about Determinism and so the Soviet power feels it is not only wise but right to welcome and patronise the physical sciences.[1] But the philosophy of Science of the Soviets is the philosophy of Science of Marx. It is not the Science of to-day, but of fifty years ago. Marxianism applied fresh and hot, the moment *Das Kapital* appeared, might have had as its base some scientific validity. Owing to the lag between making the system and applying it, that base has moved away altogether, and the scientific Determinism, which was to be the base of the complete sociology, no longer exists. Bolshevism, as an attempt to make a moral or social reply to the latest cosmological knowledge, is, therefore, no longer valid. It cannot endure argu-

[1] See also its tendentious patronage of Pavlov.

ment and so it must increasingly – as did the Church as its anthropological cosmology, the sanction of its morality was abandoned by the educated world – rely wholly on persecution. From this we can see that Bolshevism is only dangerous to those societies based on an even more inadequate foundation of fact than is the Soviet. To those who dare go on, to those who take up the appeal to truth, there is no danger in outworn dogmas. To those who dare abandon most, who dare keep open the mind longest, the future belongs.

VI

For what is that future? We have seen that man has come last to himself and that, as with psychology he suddenly perceived his motives, he saw how partial till then all his knowledge of the world had been. For a moment men felt this as the supreme humiliation. Were they not stripped of their last defence and dignity? Step by step as Science advanced man had seen himself become *pari passu* smaller. He had seemed to shrink to complete insignificance in the face of a universe as vast as it was indifferent. But he had kept his dignity. Huxley in Oxford stands as the protagonist of that stage. He has as background black space hung with uninhabitable super universes, and as a vista blank time stretching away in either direction, behind, through blind evolution down to the inertia of absolute Zero,

and in front the same blind evolution to the same
end. He stands and says, 'All that is on one side and
on the other there is I.' Certainly such a pose
cannot be said to lack dignity. And now Psychology
has taken away that dignity. Science has penetrated
not only to the bounds of space but into the foundations and springs of the mind. Men were humiliated,
they were stripped. But now we perceive that that
stripping was as necessary for man as the snake's
casting of its skin or the seed its husk. Unless a seed
fall into the ground and die it remaineth alone. Man
had to cast this final husk of his animal individual
self, its uniqueness, worth and dignity that he might
realise that man is something more than men and
that the mind which is growing in them, they do not
own and use, but it owns and uses and it is fulfilled
as it uses them up. Their complete emergence is
their assumption. There is nothing mystical in this.
It is all part of the evolutionary emergence of man.
The power of mind which made him capable of
transcending the animal outlook and of seeing,
paying attention to and understanding things in the
outer world which had for him no animal significance, that same power, by its steady growth, has
to bring him to the point where he can view himself
with the same interest and the same detachment.

The proclamation of the new knowledge was made
when Spinoza wrote his resolve not to see anything
with either approbation or disgust, but simply with
interest in it as it is. So man can see his mind

working and so at that moment he has, complementing that insight, a new and deeper insight into the world around him. He can as it were, see past the shadow cast by himself, on to a world lit by a clear shadowless light that comes no longer from his own narrow focus of interest but from a general apprehension. To some this has seemed the end. The last knot is untied, the last secret told and, see, there is nothing. The universe remains unknowable and man has only proved that it must remain unknowable, by proving that he is an instrument constitutionally incapable of detached apprehension. Man has emerged into inescapable ignorance. But this is the old mistake of early Science – it is to fail to realise that there is an onlooker, and that onlooker has gained in insight as he has won to detachment. The mind that has found out its limitations has taken the first step toward transcending them. As Dr. Santayana has said, When a man can realise his own insignificance he must be by that realisation greater than that insignificance. That this discovery of the limitations of the self, this power of the mind to interpret itself, is man's emergence on to a completely higher level of being is proved by the complementary advance of Science at the other end. Physics has not ceased advancing all the while that Psychology has been growing up. And as Psychology began to interpret man to himself, or to put it more startlingly but more accurately, as man's impersonal mind began to be able to grasp not only the universe but man in it, Physics which had so long seemed to minimise the importance of man's mind suddenly turned the corner and mind was seen again in place as the universe's centre. While the new Psychology teaches mind how to use the human mind to apprehend itself and, by 'calculating for its displacement,' as astronomers say, with that human mind to get an increasingly enlarged objective view of the outer world, the new Physics teaches that the concept called the outer world is just so much of reality as this stage of man's mind can compass and compose. We see that Physics and Psychology, the two ends of man's knowledge, now realise that each is complementary to and dependent upon the other. We have the Physics of which our Psyche is capable – we have the Psychology which is a microcosm of our Physics. Every advance in the one must be complemented by an advance in the other. The one can no more move regardless of the other than can substance move without its shadow or, a juster simile, can the body move without a corresponding effect on mind, or the mind without an effect on the body.

We are left then to-day with not only an unparalleled expansion of understanding, but with that vast field unified as men never before could conceive it being unified. That they had a subconscious hope, a faith that it would make sense, we have seen is proved by the fact that they continued to press on, continued to produce discoveries and continued to resist the temptation to cry halt or to permit authority to halt them. Now at last we see the vast expansion, the immense romantic period of modern man (and by modern man I mean all capable of Science; Greeks, Arabs, and Indians as well as Europeans since the Renaissance) beginning to co-ordinate and converge toward its 'classic period,' its secondary phase of comprehensive conclusions, and of a perfect interpretation, a completely harmonious reaction. Then the scientific cosmology will result and be fulfilled in an appropriate social action as easily and well as the Arunta cosmology is expressed in Arunta society, as easily and well as the dancer moves to a well-learnt measure. Another vast grasp and range of the outer world will have been taken and organised through another correspondingly vast expansion of man's emergent mind. He will not have complete objective knowledge even then. But he will see a complete universe because he will have lived up to the full capacity of his powers; he will have pushed to its limit, until it gave no further response, his hypothesis, his interpretative concept. He will therefore enter into his rest, another stage of his mysterious evolution completely and honestly finished. Any attempt to stop short of that completeness must end in disaster; for the mind of man will scent the insincerity, will detect the lie and, knowing that a false conclusion has been drawn, that a narrow, self-regarding, timid sham has been interposed to save men from going on to the fulfilment of their nature, that private interests have tried to fob off the need of man with a premature and sterile synthesis, his impersonal mind will give him no rest till he tears up the pretended settlement and go on again, probing, exploring, till he touch the final limit, not of present convenience but of his entire consciousness.

Then he may rest in his classic period, the greatest classic period man has ever seen. He will produce an art as beyond the art of all other ages as is the full scientific cosmology beyond that of any other time, and his conduct and the frame of his mind, his sense of others and of himself will be, must be, as harmonious and as great. Then once again the hunger for rawness, incoherence and stress will come upon this giant refreshed and completely remoulded. The limits of his universe, which seemed essential foundations, will begin to seem arbitrary and imprisoning walls. He will tire of his Eden, his Paradise of perfection, and he will fall out again into another still vaster universe there to suffer, to sorrow, to struggle, to grasp and to comprehend. So stage by stage, we can see the being in which we are, the mind which to-day as it emerges calls itself man, like a great heart, with steady beat expanding and contracting, like a great bird with steady beat rising from the earth and taking of its nature to the sky.

INDEX

INDEX

INDEX